CLASSIC TRUCKS

POWER ON THE MOVE

CLASSIC TRUCKS

POWER ON THE MOVE

Nicholas Faith

BOXTREE

In Association with Channel Four Television Corporation

First published in Great Britain in 1995 by Boxtree Limited

Text © Nicholas Faith 1995

The right of Nicholas Faith to be identified as Author of this Work has been asserted by
Nicholas Faith in accordance with the Copyright, Designs and Patents Act 1988.

1 3 5 7 9 10 8 6 4 2

Designed by Robert Updegraff
Printed and bound in Italy by Graphicom, for

Boxtree Limited
Broadwall House
21 Broadwall
London   SE1 9PL

A CIP catalogue entry for this book is available from the British Library.

ISBN 1 85283 948 1

Classic Trucks accompanies the Channel Four series 'Classic Trucks' produced by Uden Associates.

(*Half title*) As early as 1904 manufacturers of fire engines and fire-fighting equipment like Merryweather were
making mechanically-powered engines for forward-looking brigades like Finchley District Council.

(*Title page*) The chassis of the legendary Rolls-Royce Silver Ghost was strong enough to carry an armoured
body. These armoured cars were immensely useful in the Near East, the only mobile front in World War I.

CONTENTS

In the first decade of the century, the French organized rallies ('Concours') for commercial vehicles, as well as cars. Like so many other manufacturers, Panhard & Levassor made, and showed, both.

Acknowledgements

This book would never have been possible without the initiative of Peter Grimsdale and the help of Patrick Uden and his team, Maxine Carlisle, James Castle, Chris Durlacher, Caroline Hecks, Michael Proudfoot and Senara Wilson, who found the time in their hectic schedules to supply me with every bit of information they possessed. I am also indebted to them for the many (otherwise unattributed) quotations from their typescripts.

The tightness of the publishing schedule also meant heavy reliance on the expertise and sympathy of Katy Carrington and Susanna Wadeson at my publishers, Boxtree, and the skilled and imaginative designer, Robert Updegraff. My trust was fully repaid by their thoughtfulness and professionalism.

By 1924 specialist garages were equipped with towing trucks complete with cranes to rescue stranded vehicles.

Introduction

The story of mechanically-powered road transport encompasses the whole of twentieth-century history – social, economic, technical and political. A single volume can never cover the whole range of vehicles involved, from the most appealing of three-wheelers to the monsters used to haul pipelines over the Arabian sands. Moreover, the story of industrial vehicles is more than just a technical saga (though it is that as well), and a slim book like this, designed to accompany a TV series, can only hint at the many extraordinary episodes within the story which began with steam but took its final form a century ago with the development of the internal combustion engine. In that time road vehicles have replaced railways as the dominant form of land travel, and, whatever the restrictions the next century may bring, their place in the lives of the peoples of the world is secure.

This book can only illuminate the rich and various landscape with a searchlight beam, encourage readers to pursue the subject further. Above all, I hope it will lead them to look on trucks not just as machines but as a part of a human story involving their makers, their drivers, and those who rely on their efforts for their vital supplies of food and fuel – and, in the case of emergency vehicles, their very lives.

For the story of commercial transport echoes similar developments in industry and society, showing how every aspect of life has become increasingly homogenized; how individual quirks and oddities, industrial as well as social, have been ironed out in the course of the twentieth century.

As late as 1967, when I wrote a survey of the industry for *The Economist*, that process of homogenization was still by no means complete: 'The world of the commercial vehicle makers,' I wrote, 'is full of prejudices, stubborn conservatism, fierce loyalties, cut-throat rivalry, but all contained within a family speaking its own family language.' The engineers, particularly of larger vehicles, 'boast how different they are from the car makers; their products cannot, they say, be sold by a handsome salesman to a foolish housewife. They cannot be made on a production line by unskilled men. They are engineering products put together with pride and loving care by men who live with a vehicle all the time it is being assembled, in a world of men and steel resembling the car plants of forty years ago, the heyday of Ettore Bugatti and W. O. Bentley.'

I could have added that the story of these machines often reflects the national character of the producers: the French full of original ideas, most of which were unsuccessful in the short term but formed the basis of longer-term success (usually for someone else); the English dreamy and anarchic, unwilling to translate their mechanical breakthroughs into anything as vulgar as industrial success; the Americans veering between enormous originality and manic success and depression and mechanical conservatism; and finally the Germans, pursuing

(Opposite) In 1923 road transport was already quicker (and safer ?) than rail for carrying valuables to exhibitions.

11

precisely the sort of methodical, orderly, engineering-driven path which is ideal for the industry.

Even when I wrote my survey, its words were true only of heavy and specialist trucks, for vans and light and medium trucks were already being made on a mass-production basis, and since then many members of the world family have been absorbed into larger tribes: Mercedes has swallowed Saurer, the pioneering Swiss firm, as well as Freightliner in the United States (where two other proud names, Mack and White, have also passed into European ownership). In Europe Iveco was formed to group the heavy truck activities of a number of formerly proudly independent names, while in Britain the story of Leyland encompasses all the problems, from ill-judged government interference to market slumps, faced by any British firm – it is a miracle, and a tribute to the grit and the engineering skills of its employees, that it survives as an independent firm today.

But, fortunately, a handful of specialists survive, whether because, like Dennis in Britain or Oshkosh in the United States, they have found profitable market niches, or like ERF in Britain or Marmon in the United States, they are producing vehicles for a market where reliability and concern for the individual buyer counts for more than price. Such survivors reflect the general rule that in any industry, the larger the units into which the basic products are grouped, the bigger the gaps for enterprising outsiders.

Although this book, like the series it is designed to accompany, is concerned with the 'classic' vehicles of earlier generations, it is surprising to find how many ideas which are still thought quite advanced today were attempted, if not always

Acting as 'showmens' engines', hauling the rides to fairs (like this one in the historic Oxfordshire town of Thame) was the characteristic fate of ageing trucks.

successfully, from the earliest days of motorized transport. Perhaps the most obvious instance is the idea of combining electric motors with diesel or petrol engines. The use of a constant-speed engine to generate electricity to power motors housed in the hubs of the vehicle's wheels has emerged as a favourite weapon of anti-polluters because the motors can be regulated to produce minimal noxious emissions. Yet, at the turn of the century, the petrol-electric was already the trendiest of vehicles, and buses powered in this way were a familiar sight on the streets of London.

Similarly, vehicles with four-wheel drive were first made in the early years of the century, as we see on page 92, and were developed into their modern form during the first world war. As early as 1898, Thornycroft made the first articulated truck. Ten years later the London firm of Maple's was using a container-type body which could be lifted off the back of the truck and on to a railway wagon for transhipment. Even the practice of leasing vehicles, a 'modern' financial device if ever there was one, was introduced over seventy years ago by the Commercial Car Company to help customers anxious to lease rather than buy its Commer vans.

Nor is there anything new in attempts by governments to regulate and shape the industry, a matter of particular concern today with increasing awareness of pollution and the environment. Governments have tried numerous ways of taxing vehicles and their operators: they have influenced their shape and size through limits on weight and length; they have helped domestic manufacturers by bringing in import duties (the presence of General Motors and Ford in Britain is largely due to the duties imposed on imported vehicles in 1926).

In some cases they have even boosted the industry. Such help can be indirect – the minimum power-to-weight ratios imposed by the German government in the 1950s, for instance, forced the country's truck makers to make powerful vehicles which proved to be exactly what the world was looking for. Or

A perfect illustration of the problem of 'juggernauts' in old towns. This Scania 142 is hauling a bouyancy tank through the little Scottish town of Forres, in 1983.

it can be direct – the various 'subsidy' schemes described in Chapter 7 were of enormous importance in establishing vehicle industries in Britain, France and Germany.

Of course politicians only reflect public attitudes. And today, as they have always been, these are profoundly ambivalent. When a heavy truck rolls through a village street it is damned by the epithet 'juggernaut'. But when the very same trucks are used in emergencies in far-off places, they are 'lorry-loads of much-needed medical equipment'. They, and their drivers, are resigned to being treated like Kipling's archetypal soldier, Tommy Atkins: scorned in peacetime, but it's 'Thank you, Thomas Atkins, when the guns begin to roll'.

Chapter One

STEAM: ROMANCE AND REALITY

THE STORY OF the use of steam-engined vehicles for use on roads and their replacement by internal combustion engines is essentially a perverse one. As Prince Marshall puts it in *Lorries, Trucks and Vans*[1]:

The first thirty or forty years of the history of the truck is of the competition between two main approaches, the easy way and the hard way. The easy way to make a truck is to separate out all the different functions and do them in separate components. One has a furnace [boiler], into which go fuel and air and out of which comes high-temperature, low-pressure gas. One has a steam generator into which goes high-temperature gas and out of which comes high-pressure vapour. One has an expander [a cylinder], into which goes high-pressure vapour and out of which comes mechanical work. The steam engine is a classic example of the easy way to build an engine; because all the stages of turning chemical energy into mechanical work are separated, one can be stopped without stopping the others, the steam engine can start itself and its load from a standstill ... And steam engines were not only easy to understand, they were easy to build and to repair ... But very early there appeared radicals, designers who chose to do things the hard way ... For the internal combustion engine is doing in one small chamber what a steam engine requires three stages to do; it is inherently superior, albeit far harder to build; the stresses are far greater, if only because the speed of operation is ten, twenty times that of a steam engine ... The radical approach, the hard way, won out.

The 'easy way', producing steam engines designed to run on roads, had a head start. During the nineteenth century steam engines evolved into all-purpose vehicles, workhorses developed from stationary engines. As they became more specialized, they were used for hauling heavy loads for brewers and removal men, amongst others, and for such specific uses as providing power for fairground rides. On farms they did everything from drawing ploughs to providing power for balers. So it was natural for them to be used for road transport once the 4mph (6.4kph) speed limit was lifted in 1896.

Outside Britain and the British Empire, the steam-powered road-going vehicle made only a limited impact. The Americans still fondly remember the Stanley Steamer, but petrol (and electric) vehicles soon established themselves in commercial areas.

As inventors of the internal combustion engine, the Germans paid little heed to steam. Nevertheless, the Nazis, at least, shared the British obsession with using domestically-produced coal rather than imported oil as fuel. As a result, Henschel employed Warren Doble (see page 25) in the early 1930s and the firm produced steam-powered buses which ran until fuel costs escalated dramatically in 1942. Henschel even experimented with steam engines in the dark days immediately after the second world war.

A Foden unloading waste paper – surely a dangerous load for a steam truck – in Battersea, south London.

likely.

But most of their enthusiasm is romantic. As you can see from the rise of Sentinel (pages 22–25), the story of steam is one of the best examples of the British refusal to accept cold logical reality, to dream dreams – and, in many cases, turn them into beautiful machines – to prefer the byway, the blind alley, rather than drive down the broad, straight (and therefore to the true Brit, boring) road of technological progress.

The best comparison, perhaps, is with aircraft engines. It took only a few years for the jet-engined airliner to drive its propeller-driven predecessor from the skies: when the Boeing 707 was introduced in 1958 it didn't even have the range to fly non-stop from London to New York, yet twelve years later its successor, the Jumbo, was taking twice as many passengers twice as far.

Similarly, steam engines were doomed once the Germans had solved the problem of producing a diesel engine in a motor truck. The first trucks powered by diesel engines were exhibited by three German manufacturers, MAN, Daimler and Benz in 1923 and 1924. By 1928 Gardner, the British marine engine manufacturers, had produced the first of a long line of slow-revving engines with massive torque (rotary force) entirely suitable for powering motor trucks. The steam engine was dying

(Above) A ploughing demonstration at Castle Howard, in 1966, showing the classic use for a 1914 Fowler compound ploughing engine: linked by a balance plough to a similar engine on the other side of the field.

the dark days immediately after the second world war.

In Valentin Purrey the French can boast not only an interesting pioneer, but also a commercial innovator. He ran his own steam-engined bus services and in 1899 gave a dramatic demonstration of the superior productivity of steam over horsepower. The giant French sugar company, Say, set a precedent by replacing horses with steam: the thirty-four wagons Purrey delivered replaced a stable of 400 horses.

Nevertheless, the story of the steam road engine remains an overwhelmingly British phenomenon, and not only because of the country's role in inventing and perfecting steam engines to power locomotives. The supporters of steam can find rational arguments to support their enthusiasm. They will tell you that it was killed by legislation inspired by the diesel lobby (a belief which has a grain of truth in it), and that it will return because of increasing concerns about pollution, which is much less

(Right) As late as 1928, a Foden overtype was still immensely suitable for hauling a trailer.

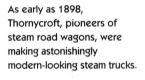

As early as 1898, Thornycroft, pioneers of steam road wagons, were making astonishingly modern-looking steam trucks.

even before Parliament gave it the *coup de grâce*.

The starting gun for motor vehicles of all kinds was fired by the 1896 Act which removed the famous 4mph (6.4kph) speed limit on Britain's roads. That year the first steam wagon, an undertype with vertical engine with compound cylinders, Number One Steam Van, was built by John Thornycroft, in the unlikely setting of a studio in Hogarth Lane in West London which also housed a famous statue of Boadicea (it had to be cast and cleared out before Number One could be built). That same year the Lancashire Steam Company of Leyland in Lancashire built a small steam van.

But it was no easy matter to build a roadworthy steam engine. Naturally enough, the first designs of the late 1890s were based on a horse-drawn dray, with a boiler mounted on the front with an engine underneath driving the rear wheels, and it took some time to refine the idea. Not every maker of steam engines could compete because most of them relied for their sales on the market for massive threshing machines used largely in East Anglia – England's granary – which is why so

many of them were located in Norfolk and Suffolk.

Over fifty manufacturers had been invited to enter the trials organized by the Liverpool Self-Propelled Traffic Association in May 1898, the event thought to mark the start of the 'steam age' on Britain's roads. In the end, though, only four vehicles entered.

Even in the 1920s, supposedly the heyday of steam, steam engines were heavily outnumbered by petrol-driven vehicles – including the 35,000 left after the first world war. By contrast, steam engines were made in tiny numbers: Yorkshire, reckoned the third-biggest manufacturer after Foden and Sentinel, made only 1,079 wagons between 1913 and 1932 (and a further three in the early 1930s), while Charles Burrell, founded in 1770, and makers of agricultural machinery since 1803, made a mere 114 overtype wagons between 1911 and 1928.

No two machines, it seems, were totally alike, yet there was one basic division. In the overtype the engine was mounted on top of a short locomotive-type boiler, just like a traction engine, while the undertype had a vertical boiler which provided far more usable space behind the engine. Yet many traditional traction-engine manufacturers stuck to the locomotive-type overtypes to the bitter end, while the undertype was the prerogative of general engineers, like Leyland, or former marine engineers such as Thornycroft and Sentinel.

At first sight this seems odd. As Maurice Kelly says in his history of the overtype engine:[2]

Looking back from 1970 it is difficult to believe that such a road vehicle could have become a commercial proposition in any era; it really required two men to control it efficiently, it had to make a stop at least once every twenty miles to pick up water, and it was out of action one day a week for maintenance. Coupled with the fact that it needed a fair-sized storage area for its solid fuel at the depot and that half its length was taken up by the power unit, it is more than amazing that it took government legislation to eventually

drive it off the road.

But at the start, the contest did not seem that unequal. As Kelly says:

The early years of the twentieth century saw many makers of obscure undertype steam wagons come and go; all of them suffered from inefficient boilers and as a result couldn't cope with hills because the boilers couldn't produce enough steam quickly enough. ...[By contrast] the overtype makers had found a wagon that could steam well on the road and wasn't fussy and temperamental.

The overtype had proved itself in generations of railway engines, so was steady and reliable. In addition, it had immense torque and could pull inordinately heavy loads – it was particularly useful for hauling pantechnicons which had

According to the publicity brochure, this 1905 five-ton Foden steam wagon 'consumed 3 ½ to 4 cwt of coal for a complete day's work, and fully loaded would climb a 1 in 7 gradient'.

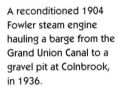
A reconditioned 1904 Fowler steam engine hauling a barge from the Grand Union Canal to a gravel pit at Colnbrook, in 1936.

originally been built to be drawn by horses.

By far the most successful manufacturer of overtypes was Foden, already a respected name in steam engines. James Sanderson, a farmer who lives near the Foden works at Sandbach, in Cheshire remembers his father saying that their threshing machines were always the best.[3]

Foden failed to produce a viable undertype and in 1900 brought out an influential overtype. Its compound engine, running at 200psi, was mounted on the locomotive boiler. It featured a gear drive to the crankshaft and final drive through chain drive to the rear wheels, and two speeds, giving 2mph (3.2kph) and 6mph (9.7kph). Twenty years later, it produced an advanced, rigid four-wheeler which could run its two chambers in any combination. This provided great flexibility and a top speed of 25mph (40kph), ample at a time when the speed limit for trucks was a mere 20mph (32kph). It featured an enclosed cab, a dynamo, flexible suspension, powerful brakes and a strong chassis, features which allowed it to be adapted for pneumatic tyres. Indeed Foden so dominated the overtype

that the design became known as 'Foden type'.

But the locomotive-type boiler was particularly troublesome in hilly regions – if it was parked on a steep gradient, the fire tubes would dry out. Hence the attempt by the Mann family to produce an engine (under the Yorkshire marque) which would be set transversely across the front. Yet the undertype was bound to win in the long run. If the failings in boiler design were cured, the wagon would be a vastly better proposition because the load-carrying platform could occupy a far higher proportion of the total length. Once the problems had been cured, progress was pretty spectacular (as can be seen by the description of Sentinel's trucks on pages 22–25).

But the distinctions were not confined to the position of the boiler. Leyland and Fowler fitted fire-tube boilers while Sentinel and Garrett made the water-tube variety. One of the joys of steam propulsion was the opportunity for experiment in the long mechanical chain between the heating of the water in the boiler and the arrival of the power at the wheels.

Manufacturers fought bitterly. Burrell offered three different

Steam engines, like this Foden being used by the City of Leicester, were ideal for filling in roads – note the covering to protect the boiler from the ash grit.

designs, all of them so influenced by Foden that the latter sued them repeatedly. Makers kept a close eye on each other. Typical was MacLaren of Leeds, most famous for the aptly named Gigantic road locomotive which it built in 1911 to haul loads of up to 130 tons. Sent to Russia to help the Tsarist army haul guns, the Gigantic ended up in Australia for road haulage. But MacLaren was just across the road from Fowler's, and the local folklore said that MacLarens were made from the bits that Fowler's threw away.

The manufacturers could afford to go to great lengths to please their customers. But perhaps the most special machines were those made for use on fairgrounds, notably by Burrell and Fowler's. The spare steam could be used to power a dynamo to provide the electricity required when the engine was stationary at the fairgrounds themselves, while the engines would drive the

rides. These 'showmens' engines' had full-length canopies supported by ornate brass curlicues and elaborate finishes, lettered and lined out in gold leaf. After up to a quarter of a century on the road, older lorries would often finish their lives on fairgrounds where the mileage was minimal and there was a lot of time available for servicing.

But more ordinary engines were just as varied. For instance, Mann's made tar-sprayers, gully-emptiers and tipping box wagons as well as the special drays which were required by two of the makers' biggest customers, namely the brewers and the millers.

The steam engine was finally killed off in the early 1930s by the implementation of the Salter Report (designed to help the railways compete against road haulage) which recommended that any vehicle which weighed over four tons unladen – a category which included all steam wagons – should face penal taxation. Responses varied. Sentinel stuck to its undertype engines while (as recounted on page 18) Foden managed to convert to diesel propulsion just in time, killing a most promising steam engine design, the Speed 6, to do so.

Two pioneers of steam, Leyland and Thornycroft, had seen the writing on the wall long before the Salter Report was written, let alone implemented, and had already switched, successfully, to petrol-engined trucks. Maudslay, founded in 1883, nearly went broke, but was saved by an Austrian refugee, Siegfried Spurling, who designed a range of diesel trucks just before the second world war.

Other makers were less adaptable. Typical were Richard Garrett, makers of the legendary Suffolk Punch tractor and thus the second-oldest engineering company in Britain, having been established in 1778. Despite the introduction of a new range of undertypes in the early 1920s, the firm went under in 1932 as part of the debacle which engulfed the Agricultural and General Engineers group and was absorbed by Beyer Peacock. William Foster, well-known makers of traction engines, made sixty overtypes after the first world war, the last delivered as late as 1933, and produced one as late as 1942 – probably the last overtype delivered to a British customer. In the event, Foster was absorbed into Gwynnes Pumps, a firm it had bought in the 1920s. Other survivors included William Taskers of Andover which switched to making trailers in 1932.

Even the mighty John Fowler of Leeds, which had been making agricultural machines since 1860, were finally killed off when the combine harvester, introduced in the 1950s, dealt a death blow to the steam-powered thresher.

Nevertheless, steam lives on in the memories of a declining band of veterans and of a larger and younger group of enthusiasts who are determined to preserve as many of these wondrous machines as possible. In the words of Joe Thomas, the historian of Sentinel: 'Steam is alive. A steam lorry is a living thing. But a diesel is dead.' When William Foden, the man who had overseen the transformation from steam to diesel in the early 1930s, died in 1964 at the age of ninety-two he was carried to his funeral by a Foden steam wagon named after his father, 'Pride of Edwin'.

STEAM: ROMANCE AND REALITY

A Foden steam wagon, 'Pride of Edwin', carrying to his grave the 95-year-old William Foden, the man who converted the family firm from steam to diesel.

THE STORY OF the Sentinel Company can be told quite briefly. The long-established engineering firm of Alley & McLennan started to produce steam engines in its Glasgow works in 1906. But the premises were too small, so in 1915 they moved to the outskirts of Shrewsbury, where they produced a series of trend-setting undertype steam wagons under the Sentinel name which were far superior to any of their numerous competitors. Production eventually reached forty-five a week, a rate unheard of in the age of steam. The works, where Sentinel made all its own parts, employed some of Britain's finest engineers, and was one of the most modern in the country. But Sentinel remained too loyal to steam and the company died in the 1950s.

But no synopsis can do justice to the tragedy of a one-time pace-setter which found itself stranded in a technological blind alley. Indeed, Sentinel's final efforts in the 1930s have all the grandeur, and the futility, of the charges made by the Polish cavalry in face of Hitler's invading Panzer divisions in September 1939.

The first great machine produced at Shrewsbury was the miraculous Standard Sentinel steam wagon. The boiler, operating at 230lb (104.32kg) per square inch, was superheated to 600°F (315.5°C). A

The Sentinel Super: note the modern styling and the short cab – and thus the long load platform – made possible by the firm's advanced undertype engine.

One of the last of the Super Sentinels, in 1935: the steam could be used for pumping, or cleaning; so steam trucks like this were in great demand from municipalities.

two-cylinder engine, theoretically rated at four tons (4.06 tonnes), could carry eighteen (18.3 tonnes). A few years later, in 1923, came the Super Sentinel, which developed 80bhp at 450rpm. With its dynamo and pneumatic tyres it could do 40mph (64kph) – double the speed limit – without causing discomfort to the driver, snug in his enclosed cab.

Four years later came the 'double-geared' model, which operated at a higher pressure than any competitor, and had a two-speed gearbox incorporated in the engine crank case. All these models were innovative and superior: for instance, they all had excellent superheaters so that they could maintain a good head of steam. Moreover, partly because of the numbers being made, the Sentinel was actually cheaper than its rivals. Customers enjoyed proper service through depots all over the country and the firm was alert to its customers' varied requirements: the Alleys produced the first-ever mobile cement mixer and for the Irish they even made one engine that would burn peat (because peat contains a high proportion of water, the engine operated at a higher temperature and was therefore more efficient than if it had been fired by oil).

Sentinel was always ready to learn. One octogenarian, Tom Ward, remembers how his father, who ran a haulage business in north Wales, used to suggest improvements to the design of the Sentinel. The Alleys would immediately patent the idea. In return, they would send round a demonstration model for the company to 'try out', though no one ever came round to collect it, or ask for payment.

But it was Sentinel's last model, the S, introduced in 1933–34, which showed what a truly sophisticated steam engine could achieve. The new four-cylinder, automotive-type engine weighed only 9cwt (457kg) yet developed 125bhp at 1,000rpm, steamed at 255lb (116kg) pressure

The great demonstration in favour of steam engines powered by British-mined coal could not halt the legislation which finally killed off the steam engine.

and was superheated to 650°F (329°C). It featured shaft drive, used for the first time on a steam engine, steam-operated brakes and pneumatic tyres. All three models – the four-, six-, and eight-wheelers – cruised at 30–35mph (48–56kph) and a fully loaded S4 could reach 50mph (80kph). Yet it could steam thirty miles (48km) on 1cwt (51kg) of Welsh steam coal and used only three gallons (fourteen litres) of water a mile, while its mechanical stoker enabled it to avoid a problem created by the 1932 Act – which decreed that if a truck was operated by one man then it would have to stop whenever the fire required attention.

In its road test, *Commercial Motor*[3] remarked on several points: the automatic stoker, the economy, the improvements thanks to shaft drive, and above all the 'uncanny facility' of the way the engine, unencumbered by a clutch, could start very gradually, with a 'standstill pull' which was extremely useful in boggy ground.

However, when the same magazine repeated the test thirty-five years later, the limits of steam traction were exposed. The tester applauded many features, like the lack of a need for clutch or sophisticated transmission and the 'surprising' degree of riding comfort thanks to the leaf springs on the front axle. And, 'from a noise point of view, compared with other vehicles of its era, the Sentinel was in a class of its own'.

But driving it was clearly an art form:

One must continually attend the needs of the steam-raising plant and I was painfully aware that the need to know one's route intimately was not confined to the ability to negotiate the various bends. More important is the need to have the right amount of steam on tap when approaching a gradient, or to know how to keep pressure down when approaching a decline.

There were also limits to the degree of driver comfort: 'One of the first things that newcomers to steamer-handling must learn is to spit first before touching anything in the cabin, for most things around the boiler are pretty hot, as I found to my cost.' Consequently, the cab was hot and suffocating in the summer (though, as one enthusiast puts it, 'toasty warm in winter').[4] So, it is not altogether surprising that a lack of skilled drivers was one of the factors that ended the steam era.

When weight limits were proposed in the new Road Traffic Act, an S4 steamed past Parliament, living up to its name of Silent Knight, to show how clean and silent steam propulsion could be, but to no avail. Yet Sentinel persisted. They hired an extraordinary American engineer, Abner Doble, one of four brothers who had built a steam car which would do 95mph (153kph) – and cost $6,000, equivalent to over $112,000 (£75,000) in today's prices. He was a perfectionist who spent five years slaving over every detail

of the ultimate steam wagon: the amazing oil-fired four-cylinder Model E.

This provided an effective answer to the two basic objections to steam propulsion: the time required to get up steam and the range. Steam was raised in a mere thirty seconds, whereas it had taken the tester from *Commercial Motor* sixty-eight minutes to get the S4 going on a fine spring morning, and the Model E could cover 250 miles (402km) on a tank of water, four times the range of the S series. But only a prototype was built before Sentinel ran out of funds. By the time production stopped later in the decade, 8,500 vehicles had been built at Shrewsbury, 7,000 of them road vehicles.

After the war, Sentinel built 100 more steamers for use as dump trucks in Argentina, and at least one old wagon was used to carry coke during the 1956 Suez crisis. But the demise of steam turned Sentinel into jobbing engineers. The firm built 1,000 diesel trucks, as well as a variety of other engines under licence. After the war, it was even reduced to producing (admittedly with exemplary efficiency) kitchen and bathroom units for prefabricated bungalows. The inevitable end came in 1956, when Rolls-Royce bought the factory and used it to make their diesel engines. Today it fulfils the same role for Perkins.

6106

Chapter Two

THE WORKHORSES

IN THE EARLY DAYS of the motorized truck industry it was by no means clear what form of propulsion would eventually win out. Some hedged their bets: in the early years of the century one entrepreneur, Sydney Straker, formed partnerships to make everything from steam wagons to petrol-driven trams. The great French pioneer De Dion Bouton also built both steam and petrol engines. With a comprehensive range (sold separately in large numbers outside as well as inside France), the firm dominated the European scene in the first decade of the century. By 1911 its 4,500 workers were making every component except the electrical equipment; there were 50,000 De Dion cars on the road and four times as many engines in other manufacturers' vehicles as well as large numbers of buses and trucks of all sizes.

But it suffered the fate of all manufacturers who supply actual or potential rivals with key components, in this instance engines. De Dion did not help its cause by overinvestment in a new luxury car, but its decline was accelerated by competition from firms which had bought its engines merely as a way of getting started before producing their own.

The petrol-electric vehicle enjoyed an early and widespread vogue. The American company Couplegear came up with the idea behind many of today's attempts to reduce pollution: a four-cylinder petrol engine providing the power for four separate independent electric motors, one on each wheel (Couplegear even provided four-wheel steering). Mercedes made a similar range which was marketed in Britain under the name Cedes. Other American entrants included Baker, which subsequently moved successfully into the manufacture of forklift trucks.

The most powerful of these petrol-electric hybrids was the road train built for the Austrian army by Austro–Daimler. This vehicle, one of whose designers was the young Ferdinand Porsche, had a generator which could produce up to 70kw. This in turn provided power for four electric motors in the hubs of the trailer's axles (the road train, incidentally, also had air-operated brakes).

By the end of the first world war, the petrol engine was triumphant – but only for a few years. In the 1920s the compression-ignition diesel engine, previously considered too slow and heavy for use in vehicles, started to come into its own.

The diesel engine as a means of propelling commercial vehicles was born in a single dramatic year, between September 1923 and December 1924. In the midst of the traumas of a currency crisis in which money ceased to have any value, the three leading German truck manufacturers, MAN, Daimler and Benz (then separate firms), all brought out their own versions of an automotive diesel. They – and the companies now included within the Klockner–Humboldt–Deutz group – had a major advantage denied to their non-German competitors: the work already done by the inventors of internal combustion engines, Messrs Daimler, Benz, Diesel and Otto, who made the first four-stroke internal combustion engine back in 1876, using

(Opposite) Leyland's works at Ham near Kingston-upon-Thames in the early 1920s. An early example of mass production. It was also used for the refurbishment of surplus army trucks bought back by the company.

In the early 1920s, commercial vehicle-makers went all out for publicity – hence this 1922 parade in the unlikely surroundings of Lincoln's Inn.

what is still known as the 'Otto cycle'.

But in 1923–24 all three German firms independently found the same way of improving the method by which fuel was injected into the combustion chamber. They had previously relied on air pressure (sometimes known as the air-blast system), but this was never going to produce adequate power from the small and compact units required to power motor vehicles. In the early 1900s Benz had evolved a pre-combustion chamber design with the help of an engineer with the picturesque name of Prosper l'Orange. On 6 March 1923 Benz decided to build the first 100 prechamber diesel engines at its works at Gaggenau in the middle of the Black Forest, previously the home of SAF (Suddeutschen Automobielfabrik), a firm absorbed by Benz in 1910. A hundred trucks were built, powered by a new diesel unit fitted with Benz's own fuel-injection pumps and nozzles. A mere five months later the first were installed in five-ton chassis and the testers were able to report that:

The engine works smoothly, is flexible and controllable, and demonstrated more than enough tractive power. Dark brown lignite tar oil was used as fuel. Consumption was about 25 percent less than in our normal petrol-engined trucks … a comparison on a demanding 103km [sixty-four-mile] course with fully laden five-tonners showed savings of 32 percent on fuel weight and 86 percent on fuel.

Daimler (still an independent firm best known for its Mercedes cars) had been developing its own range of diesel engines at its Marienfelde plant in Berlin since 1910. It steadily increased its range of engines, all of which relied on air-pressure injection, a system which had already proved successful in larger engines (including a unit which produced 380bhp at 1,700rpm). In 1921 it started production of a range of smaller units which were used initially for powering agricultural machinery. Two years later one of these – a four-cylinder unit producing 40bhp at 1,000rpm – was mounted, first in a bus and then in trucks. This – as well as a three-ton tipper – was exhibited at the Berlin Motor Show in October 1923, while Benz showed its fuel-injected engine fitted in a five-ton truck at the Amsterdam Show of early 1924.

By that time Benz had abandoned its own pumps in favour of those developed by Robert Bosch, and started to co-operate with Mercedes, which abandoned its own air-blast system well before the two firms finally merged in 1926.

MAN – which had helped Dr Rudolph Diesel to make an oil engine back in the 1890s, were not able to make a practical air-blast injection engine and also relied on the fuel injection equipment developed by Robert Bosch. The company soon exhibited a workable 45bhp five-litre engine running at 1,500rpm – very fast for the time. By 1931 MAN were offering an engine powerful enough to power a ten-ton truck.

Diesel's first impact in Britain came in 1928, when the Dewar Challenge Cup was won by a contestant using a Benz oil lorry and trailer of twelve tons which covered 700 miles (1,126km) at an average of 13.5mpg (5kpl). Contemporary petrol engines fitted in trucks could manage only 4–6mpg (1.5–2kpl).

The change-over to diesel gave a head start to manufacturers like Leyland, which had abandoned steam by the 1920s, and Thornycroft, whose board had made the courageous decision to abandon steam propulsion as early as 1907. But the development did not mean changing only the engine in a truck. The diesels were far slower revving than petrol engines, which necessitated a different type of gearbox and even a different, and heavier, chassis. Every major component had to be matched.

This is where Leyland scored: the first range of diesel engines it introduced in 1933 – and modified the next year by fitting direct injection – were interchangeable with their petrol-engined equivalents, thus greatly reducing the capital investment otherwise required to make special new chassis and bodies. Although a number of British motor manufacturers produced their own range of engines, the major engine specialists were of crucial importance because only Leyland really had the necessary resources to develop new ranges. The same was

true in the United States, where Cummins introduced their first diesel engines in the early 1930s. They set up a factory in Britain after the war and now dominate the market for engines for heavy trucks. Until recently, Perkins, which started building diesel engines in Peterborough in the 1930s, concentrated on smaller ones, but has now absorbed Rolls-Royce's diesel engine division (which was housed in the old Sentinel works in Shrewsbury).

But these firms are relative newcomers. For forty years until the mid-1970s the market was dominated by the extraordinary company of L. Gardner. For over a century and a quarter it has been based in the unprepossessing Manchester suburb of Patricroft. By 1894 it had designed and built its own oil engine and expanded into building two-stroke engines used to power fishing boats the world over, a market which the company has never lost. It was always ahead of other British manufacturers – by 1910 it had developed a spherical combustion chamber housed in the cylinder head.

In 1928 the firm's guiding light, 'Mr Hugh' Gardner, designed and built the L2, a true four-stroke direct-injection diesel (the first used on a road vehicle was installed in a bus). But it was the LW, introduced a couple of years later, which made the firm's name and formed the basis of the British commercial vehicle industry for half a century – it even enjoyed the rare honour of being made under licence in France. The LW was relatively slow and steady, virtually impossible to wear out. ('They use our engines to tow boats with Volvo engines when they break down,' Hugh Gardner once told me.)

In 1933 the lightweight, all-alloy 4LK engine was introduced and gradually developed to produce additional power (the postwar 6LXB became a favourite of bus operators in Britain and the British Empire). But Gardner's business methods were less than ideal for the post-war period. 'Mr Hugh' would not increase production rapidly, would not proceed ahead of – or even in line with – demand; and was equally slow to increase power, although in the ten years to the mid-1960s the power of the basic engine did rise from 112 to 180bhp. More power – and better gearing – doubled the maximum speed to nearly 50mph (80kph), even before 'Mr Hugh' allowed it to be turbocharged.

A major haulage firm like Baldock's would use both Garrett steam trucks and Leyland petrol-driven vehicles.

The availability of the Gardner, and of other 'proprietary' components like gearboxes and transmissions, made it easier for new entrants such as ERF. This was an offshoot of the family firm of Foden, whose story reads like a soap opera. The family was, and still is, based in the small Cheshire town of Sandbach, which their efforts (and feuds) transformed into 'Lorrytown'. The firm had been founded by Edwin Foden with the help of two sons from a first marriage, Willy and E.R. But they were pushed aside by Edwin's second wife, known in Sandbach as Black Annie, who took over control of the company after her husband's death. Helped by a team of managers, she cut all ties with Edwin's family. Willy emigrated to Australia; E.R. stayed on, saw the way the wind was blowing in engine development and designed a diesel truck, only to see the project aborted by Black Annie and her henchmen, who declared that Foden would remain steam-driven for the foreseeable future.

(Below) The Foden FG: a classic rigid eight-wheeler of the 1950s and 1960s, naturally powered by a Gardner.

(Right) Another great eight-wheeler, this time from ERF, also using a Gardner engine.

For ten months he retired to his holiday home in Blackpool but was persuaded back into business by his own son, Dennis. On his return he hired many of the old-timers who had been forced out by Black Annie and started up the company bearing his initials, ERF, just down the road from the old family firm.

His lack of capital forced him to adopt a completely different policy from the integrated operation of the family. He bought in his major components, and was lucky in that he arrived on the scene just as Gardner was introducing its first truck diesel. This policy has served the company well, and today ERF is one of the only three British-owned commercial vehicle manufacturers.

But even the original business recovered from the depredations of Black Annie and her cohorts. In the mid-1930s, Willy returned from Australia and produced the DG range, followed in the 1940s by the FG. But this was not enough to keep the firm independent during the crisis of 1979–81. Fortunately, it was bought by the American company Paccar, makers of the country's Foden equivalents, Peterbilt and Kenworth.

The diesel engine may have dominated the heavy truck scene, but it remained more expensive to buy than its petrol equivalent, an important factor in an industry where most operators were small and undercapitalized. So it made only slow and irregular inroads against other fuels, and not just petrol – in Italy in the mid-1960s there were still 40,000 vehicles powered by methane gas. In Britain in 1938 only 9,000 vehicles, less than 2 percent of the country's commercial vehicle fleet, were diesel-powered, although this included most new heavy trucks. Even in 1957 the penetration had risen to a mere 14 percent and was only a third ten years later. Its progress was impeded not only by the shortsightedness of buyers, who refused to pay the additional cost, but also by the failure of the British tax authorities to favour diesel as their continental counterparts had done.

In Britain, the arrival of the diesel coincided with the new structure for the industry created by the 1931 Transport Act, designed not only to regulate the industry but also to protect the railways from the previously unrestricted competition. This Act divided the industry into three categories. Each vehicle carried a licence: those with a C licence could carry only goods for their owners (hence the plethora of light vans discussed in Chapter Three); the B licence imposed severe limitations on both what a vehicle could carry and the radius within which it could operate while the much-coveted A licence enabled the owner to haul other people's loads wherever and whenever he pleased.

The new regulations did not destroy the cultural unity in the haulage community, which dated back to the days when such major firms as Pickford's had set up using horse-drawn carts. Although the system made life much more difficult for new entrants, it was tailor-made for the smart operators who have always proliferated in the industry. After the war abuses were inevitable, if only because business was expanding so fast. Indeed, licences became negotiable (one veteran remembers paying £2,000 ($3,000), the equivalent of £25,000 ($37,500) today, for an A licence back in the 1950s). In *The Golden Days of Heavy Haulage*[1] Bob Tuck describes some of the dodges:

A Foden DG with an early container from the (nationalized) British Road Services.

A 1934 Bedford, breaking every kind of maximum load-regulation.

You could buy a second-hand vehicle complete with its licence but the Utopian description 'General Goods – anywhere' meant paying a hefty premium. So many hauliers started off with either a contract licence, hauling for one specific customer only, or a B licence.

The industry may have been regulated, but it was not one for the weak. Until automatic gear-changes and power steering became standard fittings, driving a twenty-tonner was macho stuff. in Bob Tuck's words, 'On a sharp bend you actually had to stand up and lean over the steering column using all your arms and legs to get the leverage.' And the crash gearboxes fit-

ted until the 1960s meant that the driver had to use both skill and force to change to neutral and listen to the engine's pulse before changing gear, without losing momentum up hills (or allowing the truck to run away on the descents).

The diesel-engined trucks were less uncomfortable than their steam-driven predecessors (one veteran, Tom Ward, remembers that the steamers even lacked windows), but the forward-control cabs normal in diesels in the 1930s, where the driver sat over the engine, were desperately uncongenial. The cabs of steamers had at least been warm in winter. 'Put another bloody coat on,' was the response to one complaint about the cab of a diesel. There was no heat from the diesel engine, so in winter the driver not only needed layers of pullovers and scarves and overcoats, but also had to equip himself with a rolled-up newspaper or piece of wood to wedge the window, which invariably fell down whenever the truck ran over a pothole. One early postwar trucker remembers:

> What kept us going was the knowledge that whatever else the load just had to get delivered, there were no excuses … the load we hated most was whisky because it would get hijacked. And if it was nicked it was the driver's fault. The driver was always responsible for getting his load through on time.

Even loading was a problem: there were interminable waits at the docks to load or unload. Today, because most loads are containerized, only older drivers can manage the complicated knots required to lash the ropes over the sheeting covering the cargo. Different loads presented different difficulties: 'Fruit was a nightmare,' says another old campaigner, 'and potatoes never stayed still once you were on the road. You had to stop and adjust the sheeting.' The ropes were made of hemp, and more often than not they cut the drivers' hands to shreds and it was impossible to keep out the dirt. The result, as one unsentimental ex-driver, Peter Jeffers, recalls, 'was infection and abscesses'. He remembered the words of a German professor: 'Truck drivers have the responsibilities of a sea captain and the wages of a mate.'

> It was a hard life even in the Fifties and you had to know your craft. There were no motorway service stations; there weren't even any tea bags. We had little pellets of newspaper filled with tea leaves, sugar and condensed milk. We'd drop these into boiling water, fish out the soggy, disintegrating newspaper and drink the tea. It was disgusting but that was all you had.

Truck stops were few and far between, and some routes, especially in rural Wales, were known as starvation routes. Although this account greatly exaggerates the hardships involved, the salary and general discomfort were real enough.

One of the first Scammells capable of hauling 100 ton loads. The 80 bhp engine was harnessed to an eight-speed transmission, though 'normal' maximum speed was a mere 6mph. The man at the rear was connected with the driver 'through a loudspeaker telephone'.

In the 1950s the market was dominated by massive eight-wheelers like the AEC Mammoth Major and, above all, the Leyland Octopus. But Leyland did introduce a lighter model, the Comet, using an advanced engine designed by the Napier aero-engine company. At the time Leyland's engines, in particular, were so advanced that a number of future rivals, including DAF and Scania, took out licences for many of its design features.

Nevertheless, most British-built heavy trucks were still uncomfortable, hot in summer, noisy, slow, unturbo-charged. 'Of course, British truckers thought they were brilliant but they didn't know any better until the Europeans came along,' says one veteran. 'I've heard old boys saying how the Octopus could do 30mph (48kph) in all conditions fully laden up any hill,' reports another. 'That's just rubbish. It crawls uphill. And it's so noisy inside you need a day's rest after a day's work.'

In the 1960s everything changed, to the great advantage of the drivers, the haulage industry and its customers, but, for a variety of reasons, the British truck industry could not cope and was largely liquidated (or forced into foreign ownership) in the 1970s and 1980s.

The first shock came in the 1960s, when importers came into the market, effectively for the first time since the imposition of import duties back in 1926. Their trucks were larger, more reliable and more powerful, thanks largely to turbo-charged engines. In these the flow from the exhaust drives a turbine which pressurizes the air going into the engine (a mechanical supercharger is less efficient because it uses some of the power from the engine). Although Leyland was turbo-charging its Comet engines as early as 1955, the first offered as standard fittings were made by Swedish companies like Scania and Volvo and they, together with those of Mercedes, proved far more modern than their British equivalents.

Even Gardner lagged behind, although rather late in the day 'Mr Hugh' allowed his engines to be turbo-charged. But in 1978 his firm was absorbed by the engineering company Hawker Siddeley, which, in turn, was bought by Perkins in 1986. It is now owned by a local entrepreneur. In the process it has lost its proud position as a major engine supplier. It struggled to keep up with ever more stringent anti-pollution requirements and now largely depends on marine engines and sales of engines to countries where emission requirements are not as stringent as they are in the industrialized world.

Gardner also suffered because of their policy of only gradually increasing the power of their engines over a time when trucks were getting remorselessly bigger. While a three-tonner was once deemed a marvel, and even after the war a ten-tonner was considered a giant, it is now the government, not the manufacturers, which is limiting weights to thirty-eight tons (forty-one tonnes) to reduce wear and tear on roads. The continental trucks were not only larger, more comfortable and more modern in design, they were far more suited to the long, fast hauls made possible by the increasing network of motorways.

The Europeans were also selling into a far more open market. In 1965 the construction and use regulations were changed to increase the maximum operating weight from twenty-four to thirty-two tons (thirty-three tonnes); four-wheelers being allowed sixteen tons. Four years later, the 1968 Transport Act created a new regime which involved 'plating' to impose maximum loads, combined with annual testing, which, unfortunately, condemned many old faithfuls to the

The AEC Matador was a favourite of the military – and of civilian hauliers in rugged country.

This Leyland eight-wheeler had to be reliable. If it broke down the liquid glucose would cool down and solidify.

scrapyard. The legislation introduced operator licensing and abolished the old distinctions overnight.

All these developments came about during a decade which brought Leyland to its knees. It was already suffering from the introduction of the Ergomatic cab: this was originally hailed as a major advance, but was far too small to contain the driver and the engine of the heavier trucks with any degree of comfort. And in 1968 Leyland was forced by the Labour government to take on the hopeless task of salvaging the British Motor Corporation, the ill-fated merger of Austin and Morris which was effectively bankrupt.

Lack of resources and management attention led to the introduction of an underdeveloped, and therefore unreliable, series of engines: the 500. Leyland fought back with the Marathon and then with a totally new design in 1980, the Roadtrain, deservedly voted Truck of the Year by the international motoring press. But the endless restructurings of the 1970s, combined with the ball

and chain of the motor-car business, dragged Leyland down and it finally ended up in an unequal merger with its former licensee, DAF. Fortunately, much of it has now been rescued from the clutches of the Dutch firm, which itself went broke in 1991.

Overall, the decline in the industry has been steady and remorseless. Nearly fifty manufacturers emerged in the first decades of the century. At the end of the second world war there were still twenty-seven. Many were caught up in the series of mergers which created the ill-starred British Leyland combine, including nearly fifty once proudly independent firms, ranging from Maudslay to Bean's, a company once famous for its cars which had become a foundry business. But the original scene had been too chaotic, too fragmented for the mergers, unlike those in Germany or even in France, to save the industry. By 1981 there were only eleven manufacturers; now there are only nine, of which only three, ERF, Dennis and the remains of Leyland triumphantly snatched from the receiver, are British-owned.

DAIMLER AND BENZ: THE TRIUMPHANT PIONEERS

IT IS ALMOST UNIQUE for the pioneers in any industry to be still in business 100 years later, let alone to dominate it worldwide. Yet Daimler and Benz, founded in 1896, are now the biggest producers of commercial vehicles in the world. Throughout their history, first as two separate firms and then, since 1926, as a single, integrated concern, they have offered the whole range of commercial vehicles, not just general-purpose trucks and buses under the Mercedes name first used for Daimler's cars, but also the very different vehicles required for fighting fires, clearing sewers – all the highly varied tasks treated separately in this book. The company's omnipresence in the market, like its history, makes it unique. The achievement has been the greater because the two firms' factories were almost all reduced to rubble as a result of Allied bombing in the second world war.

Gottlieb Daimler and Karl Benz had produced the first motor cars powered by internal combustion engines in 1886 and by the turn of the century both were producing commercial vehicles. In September 1896, Daimler and his designer colleague William Maybach introduced the world's first motor truck. Indeed they presented a complete range, with gross weights from 1,500kg (one and a half tons) to 5,000kg (five tons) powered by a range of two-cylinder engines producing from 4 to 10hp. Their engines apart, these were not advanced vehicles: their iron-shod wheels were wooden, and the driver sat on a wooden bench while operating a vertical steering column. However, the suspension did feature coil springs on the rear axles and leaf springs on the front. In 1898, Benz, who had produced a petrol-engined eight-seater bus two years earlier, made his first commercial vehicle – a delivery van with a payload of 600kg (12cwt) which he sold to an American firm for delivering goods around New York.

That year Daimler installed their first Bosch magneto ignition in a truck and followed Benz on to the overseas markets which appreciated their efforts earlier than their compatriots. In the United States Gottlieb Daimler was already working with William Steinway, the piano manufacturer, who produced their vehicles for some years. Daimler also succeeded in selling numbers of delivery vehicles in the USA (enough to require the establishment of the world's first truck service centre in Philadelphia). But a disastrous fire, followed by America's entry into the first world war stopped the firm dead in its tracks. Nevertheless, the principle had been established: where British (and, to a lesser extent, French) manufacturers depended on underdeveloped, captive, imperial markets for their overseas sales, Daimler and Benz were at their strongest in the most sophisticated countries.

Daimler's lead was most obvious in Britain. This was the result of the success of the so-called

One of the first post-buses delivered by Daimler's Marienfelde works, in Berlin to the Bavarian Post Office, which used it to carry passengers as well as mail.

Milnes lorries in the truck trials held in Liverpool in 1900. They were built at Daimler's Marienfelde factory in Berlin, whose previous owners had been associated with G.F. Milnes, a London firm of tramcar manufacturers, since 1897. This joint venture had been arranged by Frederick Simms, who held the rights for the firm's products throughout the British Empire. A year later, the General Post Office bought a Daimler, a success which led to the acceptance of the marque, for use as postbuses as well as for deliveries, by the Bavarian post office in 1905. But probably its most famous products were the buses it sold in London through Milnes–Daimler. These were built in the company's factory in Tottenham Court Road, in the heart of London, which also produced a wide variety of vehicles from tippers to fire wagons. Other customers included the City of Glasgow, which bought Daimlers for street cleaning in 1902 and went on to acquire their buses.

Another major market for the firm was the Austro–Hungarian Empire, which was deemed so important that Paul Daimler (son of Gottlieb, who died in 1900), was put in to manage it. Austro–Daimler manufactured some of the world's first four-wheel drive vehicles, big tractors with engines producing up to 90hp, as well as an advanced and popular general-purpose truck with a four-cylinder 12hp engine and shaft drive.

But Marienfelde set the pace, benefiting from the German army's subsidy scheme (see page 85) but also offering a newly developed fire engine and other advanced vehicles. These included a tipper built for the Russian market with one of the first propeller shafts and rear-axle differential and, in 1916, a two-ton lorry for Schenker & Co., probably the first international road transport vehicle.

As early as 1888, Gottfried Daimler had patented a petrol-driven fire engine, though consumer conservatism meant that the first was only delivered in 1906. This one, another Marienfelde product, dates from 1907.

Despite the starring role played by both firms in the development of a diesel engine suitable for trucks (a revolution described on pages 27–29) the postwar slump and subsequent hyperinflation – during which Marienfelde was reduced to merely repairing vehicles – led to the Daimler–Benz merger in 1926. This early partnership was in sharp contrast to the fragmented scene in Britain, where a similar process took a further forty years to complete. By 1931, Daimler–Benz was in a unique position: unlike its smaller and more specialized British and American competitors it could offer a comprehensive range of vehicles (the L series) with payloads ranging from 1,500kg (one and a half tons) to 6,500kg (6.4 tons) and with either diesel or petrol engines, ranging from a four-cylinder

45bhp unit on the 1,500kg model to a six-cylinder diesel on the 6,500kg L6500.

The group prospered as the arrival of Hitler to power generated an economic recovery – and an ever-increasing demand for military vehicles – production rose fivefold to 10,000 trucks in the three years 1932–35. The construction of the new network of autobahns also helped encourage the production of fast, advanced vehicles such as a streamlined coach powered by a 95hp diesel and capable of reaching 115kph (71mph).

The Daimler–Benz factories were natural targets for Allied bombers during the second world war, although the Mannheim factory was spared because the Americans wanted to use it as a repair centre for their own trucks. As the board of directors put it: 'Daimler–Benz ceased to

A cab-over engine five-tonner made at Benz's Gaggenau works in the Black Forest, between 1906 and 1910.

exist in 1945,' a date known in Germany as 'Year Zero'. Problems ranged from a lack of communication between the factories to restrictions, not lifted until 1951, which prevented any German company from building trucks with more than two axles (although this particular limitation was circumvented by the use of a couple of trailers).

But the firm's postwar recovery was amazing. The old Benz factory at Gaggenau was back in limited production in September 1945, although it had been bombed to blazes a year earlier. Three years later it started production of one of the firm's truly original ideas, the four-wheel drive Unimog, a robust 4x4 pick-up and small truck for use in rough country. Although it lacked the general appeal of the Land Rover, it ensured that Mercedes was properly represented in this market. At the Hanover trade fair the following year Daimler–Benz presented its first new postwar range, from the L3250, a three and a half-tonner with a six-cylinder diesel engine developing 90bhp (a model known as the 'fast truck'), up to the L6600, with a 145hp diesel.

The mid-1950s saw a change from the previous normal-control, bonneted designs to forward-control models, known as 'Pullmans' in German. At the same time the firm introduced an exhaust brake as standard equipment. By then it was well on the way to its present dominating position. The company's export drive had started in earnest in 1950, and was greatly helped by two requirements imposed by the Federal German government (which also brought in restrictions designed to help the country's railway system). First of all, the government specified the world's first minimum power-to-weight ratio which, indirectly, ensured

that all Mercedes trucks would have adequate power to tackle the roughest of roads the world over. Then, in 1956, the government imposed limits on axle weights, thus leading to a concentration on two separate types of vehicle: lighter two-axle rigid trucks and heavier three-axle types, designed to act as a tractor for a total weight of twenty-four tons. The sales of the heavier models were helped by the 200bhp motor, which was well above the minimum 6bhp per ton required by law. Mercedes were further helped by a rise in maximum weights at the end of the decade.

In 1969 the company filled the only real gap in its product range when it bought the combined Hanomag–Henschel business, which had itself absorbed the long-established makers of the Matador and Viking marques of light commercial vehicles six years earlier. Until the takeover Mercedes had been virtually unrepresented in the enormous market for vehicles of under four tons.

Mercedes has never looked back. In the 1980s it even conquered its last peak, the United States market for heavy trucks, with the acquisition of Freightliner (see pages 24–25). Even in a bad year like 1993 it produced nearly a quarter of a million trucks, far more than any of its competitors. The only danger is the ever-increasing premium price paid by all German manufacturers for producing in the motherland rather than in other industrialized countries, most notably the United States, where the cost of labour is so much lower than at home.

And the keys to the firm's success? Well, there's the solid tradition of German engineering excellence, but perhaps even more important has been the solidarity, the team spirit, and the fact that since the death of the founding fathers early in the century the firm has never been dominated by a single charismatic personality.

Daimler's production in the boom of the 1930s, generated by Hitler's rearmament programme, was concentrated on its L-Range, like this 6.6 tonner.

Chapter Three

HELPERS IN THE HIGH STREET

MOTORIZED VEHICLES, powered by electricity as well as by petrol engines, were immediately welcomed by manufacturers and retailers needing to deliver their goods. As cities spread geographically, so did the need for small-scale deliveries over increasingly long distances. Major manufacturers used the vehicles for delivery to their smaller retail customers; wholesalers used them for rushing perishables from the market to the shops; even the railways found them extremely useful (in particular the Scammell Scarab, see page 56). Department stores used them in cities, as did even the lowliest retailer in small towns, particularly in the commuter belts around London. Though the trend was universal, they are chiefly remembered for the service they provided for the shops' individual customers. By 1912 Harrods had sixty-three Albions and Whiteleys, another then-famous store, had twenty-two. Between them they covered over a million miles. One of Benz's first orders was for delivery vans to be used by New York department stores. By 1928 the biggest firm of undertakers in France had 300, while the wine merchants Nicolas had nearly 200, and the makers of Javel disinfectant, Lesieur oil and the grocer Felix Potin each had over 100.

In Britain such vehicles are indelibly associated with a certain type of civilization: the middle-class suburban housewife of the period between the wars. These vans and lorries, specially designed for every conceivable use at a time when home delivery was the norm for most middle-class households, were the street slaves of Britain for half a century. There were vans for the shopkeepers selling perishable goods in the days before refrigeration (let alone freezer cabinets): the grocers, greengrocers, butchers, bakers and fishmongers. Rather larger lorries were used by the merchants delivering coal, paraffin and oil, and, more humbly, there were tricycles for 'Stop me and buy one' ice-cream peddlers.

These commercial vehicles were distinguished sometimes by their strange shapes, and, more usually, by their lovingly crafted hand-painted signs, for the history of the delivery van is also part of the history of advertising. The vans could have come straight out of Toytown, they might have been operating in a demure Arcadian setting, but the high streets had become a parade ground of mobile advertising slogans, including some of the brashest publicity experiments ever seen – even Rolls-Royces and Bentleys were used to advertise such mundane products as Englebert tyres and Seager's Gin.

(Opposite) In the 1940s Bedford was king of the light-truck market.

Major department stores,
like Harvey Nichols,
remained faithful to electric
delivery vans long after this
picture was taken in 1922.

Rollers, however, were the exception rather than the rule. The shops' requirements were originally met by the thousands of demobilized ex-servicemen who bought war surplus lorries – Leylands, Thornycroft and Albions. These were cheap and robust but heavy and clumsy.

In the 1920s manufacturers turned their attention to this promising market. By 1928 the country possessed a fleet of nearly 150,000 vehicles capable of carrying between 12cwt (610kg) and a ton. By this time there remained only a handful of electrically-driven rivals, which survived only as delivery vans for some department stores and as milk floats.

The pioneers included makers of heavier vehicles trading down and manufacturers of medium-sized cars, but the biggest impact was made by the Bullnose Morris and, to a lesser extent the van version of the tiny Austin 7. The tradition continued into the 1930s, when manufacturers like Morris took full advantage of the separate and self-supporting chassis used in cars to convert them to small vans.

But there was one, inevitably much-loved, eccentric: the Trojan. This was described by many – and not unjustly – as '- weird', 'ugly', 'unique' and 'just plain horrible'. Originally designed as a car, in van form the vehicle was built for some years by Leyland at its London factory but later was made by an independent concern. The Trojan had a unique four-cylinder two-stroke engine, lodged under the driver's seat, which produced a mere 10hp and uttered an unmistakable bleating sound. Even in the 1920s many of its features, like chain drive, solid tyres and hand starter, were outmoded, but it continued in production into the 1930s. It survived thanks to its price (a mere £157 10s – $236.25 – complete), its ease of maintenance (the engine had only seven moving parts – four

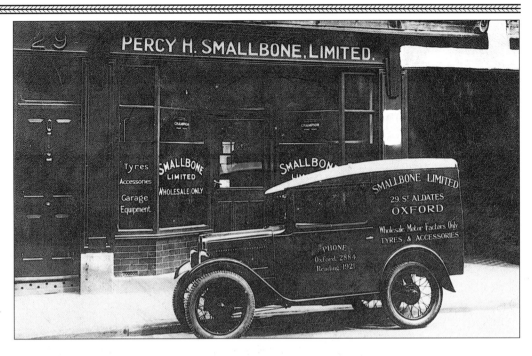

(Above) The tiny Austin 7 was ideal for small firms like this Oxford wholesaler.

(Left) The indescribably ugly Trojan was greatly appreciated by small shopkeepers because it was cheap and reliable.

By 1922, every type of
power was in use: horses,
petrol engines – including
electric vehicles used by
major railway companies
like the London and
NorthWestern.

pistons, two forked con-rods and a crankshaft), gradual improvements and the fidelity of one very important customer, Brooke Bond Tea.

During the 1920s in this sector, as in so many others, vehicles became more specialized. The Morris Commercial 'tonner' made a considerable impact, replacing the Model T Ford as the most widely used medium-weight van. It was cheap to produce, easily repaired and was made at the then amazing rate of 300 a week. But it soon faced competition from Ford and General Motors, who had been forced to start manufacturing their vehicles in Britain after a 33⅓ percent import duty was imposed in 1926. This stopped the flood of vans from such makers as Reo in America and Unic in France, which sold a lot of taxis in London.

In the early 1930s Bedford introduced a two-ton van with a modern six-cylinder 26.3hp engine. These 'British Bedfords' lived up to their slogan 'You see them everywhere.' They set the standard, so much so that their Austin-made rivals were known as 'Birmingham Bedfords'. Around the same time the synchromesh gearbox was first used in commercial vehicles, by Vauxhall. These were far easier than the old crash-type box.

The trend towards buying a van rather than a suitable type of car, persisted until the 1960s as a result of the postwar purchase tax of up to 45 percent imposed on cars, from which vans were exempt. This tax was a severe disincentive to manufacturers to come up with a vehicle that would combine both jobs.

It was different outside Britain, not only for tax reasons, but also as a matter of class distinction – the British middle classes would not be seen dead in a van, which marked its owner as being 'in trade'. By contrast, the pick-up truck was the badge of the self-employed American, while in other countries economics dictated the pattern of ownership. In Italy shopkeepers could not afford vans so they used tiny Fiat Giardinieras. In France the Citroen 2CV was introduced in the 1930s to act as a dual-purpose vehicle on the rough roads of the French countryside. In the 1950s the even more popular and almost equally long-lived Renault R4 filled the same role. This car was to become immensely popular in Britain as the country started to become less class-conscious in the 1960s.

By that time, the golden age of home delivery was a mere memory, for it had ended with the onset of war. During the war years, and for a long time afterwards, there was simply not the fuel available, and by the time the shortages had disappeared the middle classes had started to shop for themselves, and to an increasing extent in supermarkets. Home deliveries continued, but only for a few commodites, notably milk.

The vans themselves became standardized, mass-produced items. In the early 1950s Bedford produced the CA – the first panel van mass produced in this country, complete with semi-forward control and sliding doors. But Ford dealt the final death blow to non-conformity in 1962 with the Transit. This spelled a new era of international integration because it resulted from the first collaboration between the firm's British and German subsidiaries. It was intentionally made wider than the vehicles it replaced. ('A van that wide will never sell,' said the salesmen – they were wrong.) This was a deliberate step to accommodate the front-mounted V-8 engine in response to the customers' basic demand, which was for maximum space.

Other manufacturers followed suit, emphasizing above all accessibility – the Danes bought vans with right-hand drive, even though they drove on the right, so that the driver could hop out quickly straight on to the pavement. Hence the spate of 'walk-thru' vans, though these could not be sold in Germany, where access from the cab to the rear was forbidden.

But the Transit set the pace and by 1985 two million had been sold in 500 versions, including the first integrated motor caravan and a people-mover (Kombinationskraftwagen), a throwback to the early days when any suitable chassis was used for what would now be termed a 'minibus'. It was respectable enough to be bought by a French undertakers who used it to carry corpses as distinguished as that of President Pompidou who died in 1974. By that year the tradition of home delivery was virtually moribund, even in Britain – apart from the immortal milk float – and the vehicles were kept going only by a handful of prestigious stores, such as Harrods, and by companies using them for advertising purposes.

(Opposite) An early Bedford (over)loaded with the kit bags of the cadets from HMS Worcester.

The Model T Ford, a sturdy and substantial vehicle, was ideal for delivering beer (*opposite*) groceries (*right*) – or Brazil's famous sausages (*below*).

The 'Municipal and Dustcart' Business

The authorities who run the world's towns and cities have always been much-prized customers for the handful of firms able to cope with their very specialized municipal requirements – the removal of rubbish, water or sludge, for example. Commercial vehicles collect dustbins, sweep the streets, sprinkle them with water in summer, clear the snow in winter, and empty gullies and sewers throughout the year.

By 1904 the Paris authorities were using a mechanized water-carrier to damp down the dust in the magnificent Avenue Foch five times a day. 'The machine sprays an immense jet of water and moves between the lines of vehicles

with extraordinary ease and rapidity,' noted one contemporary observer.[1] Eight years later the Parisian authorities defined the specification for a specialized refuse collector: among other requirements it had to be low for easy tipping, which was difficult with a traditional high rear axle.

One solution was an Italian system of electric propulsion, which incorporated the world's first power steering. But by 1911 De Dion-Bouton had designed a special vehicle with a dropped chassis to prevent dustmen from having to lift their loads above their heads. In other countries, too, the major manufacturers made sure of their place in the market. Also in 1911, Benz made

As late as 1936, councils like Westminster were still using Foden steam wagons for ripping up the old wooden setts.

BRL 787

By 1936, specialist tippers were being replaced by machines based on standard commercial chassis like this Bedford.

a self-propelled vehicle with a steam disinfecting chamber, while in the 1930s its L series trucks could be supplied with an apparatus for sweeping, washing and sprinkling streets.

In Britain, needless to say, the market was dominated by smaller specialists. There was even room for steam-powered machines: the famous gully-emptiers made by Mann's and John Fowler were bought by municipalities all over the country. In the words of Maurice Kelly,[2] this versatile coke-burning machine 'was capable of emptying, cleansing and resealing street drains, emptying cesspools, street washing and sprinkling'. The engine could supply steam or hot water for cleansing purposes and create a vacuum for use as a pump. It was a star of the 1920s but, like every other steam-powered vehicle, it became a victim of the diesel engine.

The pioneer of the special municipal vehicle, however, was the long-forgotten firm of Lacre. It stumbled on the idea of supplying mechanical roadsweepers to town councils which had previously relied on crude adaptations of ordinary truck chassis. Lacre were asked to adapt one of their well-known O-type two and a half-ton chassis and decided to provide a special vehicle. It was cheap to buy and economical to run. It also had a single steered rear wheel and a small turning circle which meant that it could get its broom into the most inaccessible spots, while the broom itself gave a good breadth of sweep. This machine saved Lacre in the difficult years after the first world war, but unfortunately, their chief engineer, James Drewry, left in 1922 to found his own company.

A year later, Drewry and his partner, Harry Shelvoke, produced a very advanced solid-tyred small-wheel truck they had developed while working for Lacre. Its platform was a mere 2ft (61cm) above the ground and it had a turning circle of only a few feet. Forward control allowed good use of space for its two-ton load – the driver and his tiller steering were perched ahead of the front wheels and above the transverse engine. The three-speed gearbox incorporated a right-angle drive to a live rear axle through an open propeller shaft. The machine and its successors became synonymous with the rubbish collection market, but the firm faded away in the 1960s. The only survivor of the specialists is Dennis, which has always had a special division to advise on and supply the purpose-built vehicles.

(Opposite) It was typical of Mack to produce a dustcart this massive.

55

THREE WHEELS GOOD

(But in the End Four Wheels Better)

THREE-WHEELERS HAVE disappeared from the roads of the developed world and are now associated with the teeming slums of third-world cities. They were much less out of place in the days before the second world war when motorcycles and sidecars were often used for delivery purposes. Three-wheelers came in many varieties: in Germany the Phanomobil was a bestseller; in the United States the Wisconsin company designed a similar, chain-driven machine for finding its way round the crowded Chicago stockyards. But Britain was the true home of these eccentric vehicles.

They included the 'cycle carriers' like Walker and Portwine, who made 'Autocarriers' and, in a later incarnation, became AC Cars at Thames Ditton. The most successful of the three-wheelers was Scammell's Mechanical Horse (there had been others but the name became associated with the most successful of the type). It was originally designed by Napier, the aero-engine manufacturers, but they soon handed over the project to Scammell, which introduced it in 1933 as a replacement for the Cob three-wheeler. It featured gearing which gave very big reduction (between 13–1 and 23–1 for the six-tonner and 10–1 to 28–1 for the three-tonner). This provided enormous torque but a light which came on when the road speed went above 18 mph (29kph) ensured that the vehicle was slow. Its crucial advantage was the automatic coupling gear with coupling hooks, two ramps and an undercarriage. This made the machine a favourite of the railway companies because it could exchange trailers so quickly – even the tractor's rear light automatically connected once the trailer had been disconnected. But it was a pretty basic vehicle without a self-starter, the seating position (which was non-adjustable) was fairly upright and the instrumentation consisted merely of an ammeter.

Moreover, says Bill Aldridge: 'Due to the offset engine position [it had] an annoying propensity to "fall over" on sharp right-hand turns.'[3]

Nevertheless, it proved immensely popular, as did its postwar successor, the Scarab, named, not for the beetle which it resembled, but from the words *Scammell* and *Arab*, the best breed of horse. In the late 1950s, however, British Rail's delivery patterns changed and although it could be coaxed up to 55mph, it was simply too slow.

There is one survivor from the golden age of the three-wheeler, the Reliant. This was first produced by the three-wheel department of Raleigh Cycles. In 1935 the division was sold to one T.L. Williams. Many of the components he inherited had 'R' for Raleigh stamped on them so he used Reliant, a name beginning with the same letter, for his vehicles. The tradition of three-wheelers he inaugurated (originally with engines from the Austin 7) is still going today.

From 1930 (the date of this picture), Scammell three-wheelers were used by railways to haul container-loads of freight from sidings to the customer, and continued well into the 1960s when the railways no longer hauled many small loads.

Chapter Four

ALL ABOARD

IT ALL STARTED in 1823 in the French town of Nantes when a M. Stanislaus Baudry ran a horse-drawn bus to his hot baths from a stand outside the shop of one M. Omnes, advertising the service with the phrase, 'Omnes Omnibus'.

Omnibus services spread to major cities, but remained horse-drawn until the early 1900s because, generally speaking, steam buses proved impracticable – they were too slow, too heavy. Indeed, if the petrol engine had not come along the electric tram might have remained the dominant form of urban transport this century – it is now making a comeback under its new name of 'urban light railway'. In the meantime, the bus took over for humdrum everyday activities like going to work, while the '-coach' implied much more glamorous and exciting journeys such as going on holiday.

Although Gottfried Daimler built a bus as early as 1894, the first proper bus service was probably that inaugurated in 1897 which ran between Courbevoie, just outside Paris, and Colombes. It used a Scott's steam traction engine to haul an engine and coach together carrying thirty-eight passengers. Unfortunately, the engine gave up the ghost after a mere fourteen months. Other pioneering bus services in the Normandy countryside financed by the Comte de Dion* came across a problem which was to become all too familiar: they were overcrowded on market days, empty at other times.

The development of bus services in London and Paris soon diverged. Paris started with the double-deckers they called '*à l'Imperiale*' but soon turned to single-deckers. The distances in Paris are much shorter than in London and a single-decker was more practical. Moreover, in Paris, the seating upstairs was half the price of seats inside so the top decks became overcrowded and the buses unstable. This did not stop the French sneering at the British for being backward in sticking to the double-decker.

London was naturally the source of the biggest single orders but, as can be seen on pages 72–77, the city soon developed its own style of buses. The first municipal bus service in Britain using petrol-driven vehicles was not in fact set up in the capital, but in Eastbourne, when four fourteen-seat Milnes–Daimlers inaugurated a service on 12 April 1903. The bus was the product of an alliance between a young engineer, Frederick Simms, who had bought the British rights for Daimler engines as early as 1893, and G.F. Milnes, a well-known tram manufacturer.

The Milnes–Daimlers proved popular. Their most famous model, one of the first purpose-built buses not based on a horse-drawn original, was introduced in February 1904 at the Crystal Palace Motor Show. It was a simple beast, with a 24hp Daimler engine mounted in front of the driver, cast steel

(Opposite) By 1925, buses, mostly owned by the London General Omnibus Company ('The General'), were causing jams in London's Oxford Street.

wheels, a constant mesh gearbox and chain drive, which was soon replaced by a differential-type back axle. Its success proved timely for Milnes, as their tram-building business was about to go into liquidation.

For a time the petrol-electric bus appeared to offer a serious threat to the pure petrol vehicle. The most famous were those made under the name Tilling–Stevens. Naturally they were much easier to drive than an orthodox machine: the separate electric motor attached to each wheel meant there was no need to change gear. Unfortunately, the motor was generally not powerful enough to provide adequate power for climbing hills, and at a time of inadequate braking systems, the engine could not be used as a brake when the bus was descending a gradient.

By the end of the first world war the manufacturers had a range of pretty reliable vehicles to offer. They were relatively cheap to buy and were also available on easy credit terms. But, as John Hibbs[1] points out:

All this supply potential would have been useless without sufficient effective demand. Before the war the industry had been largely engaged in providing a substitute for the horse bus in towns and cities...the new potential of the industry was matched by a corresponding demand for its services and

the stage was set for expansion on the grand scale. By the end of the decade, the network of bus services that we have today had been established; the express coach service had appeared from nowhere and the whole economy of inland transport had been transformed. At the same time the motor bus had ceased to be an obvious adaptation of the horse bus and the charabanc had become obsolete with the development of the touring coach.

There were 331 operators in 1916 and nearly 4,000 by the end of the 1920s. The newcomers, operators and drivers alike included former 'carriers' and, indeed, anyone who liked the freedom offered by the job. The result was a lively regionally based industry with strong local traditions. One example was the famous Southdown company. This was founded in Worthing in 1915 and spread right through the southern counties over the succeeding decades. The early names remained strong: In Cheltenham until recently they talked of 'going to London on the Black and White', even though they would be travelling on a coach run by, say, National Express.

During the 1920s operators grew steadily more ambitious as the memory of the dreadful crash on Handcross Hill (see page 62) faded. The first truly regular express service was inaugurated by Greyhound Services between London and Bristol on 11 February 1925, although Southdown had already been operating an express bus service between Brighton and London for a year. Within three years there were four different operators running buses between Edinburgh and Newcastle, for instance, by four different routes. It was a time of seemingly limitless expansion for the companies with slightly overblown names (Majestic Saloon Coaches, National Coachways) and even individuals, like Mr F. Taylor of Middlesbrough, who ran the Blue Band Bus Service from his native town to London. Sleeper coaches were introduced on the route between London and Liverpool in 1927 and between London and Newcastle the next year though, said the brochure, 'full undressing was not permissible'.[2]

By 1930 there were 128 operators running such services (with many more taking on holiday traffic). There were twenty in the Isle of Thanet alone and nearly as many in Portsmouth and other seaside areas. The holiday market was a natural for express coach services. In 1910 Chapman's of Eastbourne advertised a tour of north Wales using a twenty-two seater Dennis bus and by 1920 they were organising six-day tours of the French battlefields (almost certainly the first continental coach tours). By the early 1920s Motorways, founded by H.J. Spencer and Graham Lyon, a remarkable pioneer who subsequently built the first motels in the country, were running as far as Belgrade and north Africa.

In Britain the operators' progress was matched by that of the builders, even though the builders were hampered by the fact that their customers, the operators, felt they had the necessary expertise and knowledge of local conditions to provide their suppliers with different detailed specifications. As a result few

In 1905 Vanguard pioneered bus services between London and Brighton. But a year later, the Handcross Hill accident set the cause of long-distance bus travel back for decades.

A SIDE VIEW OF THE WRECKED 'BUS.

THE "STRIPPED" FLOOR.

THE SHATTERED TOP OF THE 'BUS, WHICH WAS THROWN OVER THE HEDGE NEAR THE POINT OF COLLISION.

THE TREE AGAINST WHICH THE 'BUS STRUCK, AND SOME OF THE WRECKAGE.

First, and most famous, of bus accidents. The 'Handcross Hill disaster' of 1906 cost ten lives – and rated a whole page in the *Illustrated London News*.

ON 12 JULY 1906 a 'Vanguard' Milnes–Daimler, similar to the buses used on the Brighton services, was on its way to Brighton with a private party from Footscray and Orpington [in Kent]. About 200 yards (183m) down the hill, the cardan shaft broke away from the casing of the gearbox, thus breaking the transmission between the engine and the wheels and preventing the driver from using the compression of the engine to assist normal braking. To stop the vehicle running away he tried to steer into the bank, choosing the offside of the road. But the heavy camber gave the bus a severe tilt and the upper-deck passengers were swept into the road by the branches of a tree, ten of them being killed. The bus itself was so stable that it came to rest still upright some thirty yards further on, at right angles to the road.

Public confidence in the idea of long-distance bus services was shaken by the disaster, although country services that ran just the same risk were not affected … The combined effect was to delay the appearance of the express coach for some twenty years.[3]

buses were sold 'off the shelf' apart from the Bristol OB petrol-engined coach. Thus in Britain – and in Britain alone – the bodywork, the chassis and the engine were independently designed and produced in custom-built packages. Even at Leyland, where all three were produced on a single site, the three workshops were kept separate to give the impression that they were independent.

In 1925 Leyland, soon to emerge as the country's leading bus manufacturer, was able to make a considerable impact with the L range. Of the five models on offer the outstanding success was the Lion. This was a single-decker chassis with an overhead-valve four-cylinder 5.1-litre petrol engine and a double-reduction rear axle which gave out a distinctive whine. Crucial to its success were the pneumatic tyres fitted to a later variant, the PLSC1, of which more than 2,500 were produced.

It was only the arrival of pneumatic tyres which provided the comfort to enable buses and coaches to escape from their previous role as mere adjuncts to the railway services. As Hibbs[4] says: 'The importance of tyres cannot be overestimated.'

Early buses had to be shod with steel because solid rubber (the only alternative available at the time) was so expensive. At first the wheels were made of wood, but these shrank and so cast-steel wheels were fitted as standard on London buses by 1910. The first pneumatic tyres were fitted as standard in 1927 to the buses run by Wolverhampton Corporation and by 1928 they were being used by AEC on the NS buses operating in London (see pages 73–76). Only with pneumatic tyres could the industry take advantage of the government's relaxation of the speed limit when it raised the maximum from 12mph (19kph) to 20mph (32kph) in 1928.

Leyland's double-decker equivalent of the Lion was the Titan TD1, which was introduced at the 1927 Olympia Motor Show. The first to be designed from the start to run on pneumatic tyres, the Titan was probably the first vehicle to compete seriously with the speed and comfort offered by the electric tram. 'When you bury a tram,' ran one famous advertising slogan, 'mark the spot with a Titan.' It immediately acquired star status, thanks to its sleek appearance and its excellent

In the 1930s, Essex was still rural and the roads appropriately primitive.

springing, combined with its 6.8-litre six-cylinder overhead camshaft petrol engine, its four-speed sliding mesh gearbox and a standard low-loading body seating forty-eight passengers. By 1929 most Titans were equipped with enclosed staircases. It was used by a dozen major fleets like Alexander's, Southdown and Ribble. The Titan continued in production for twenty years and successors of the same name also earned the slogan applied to the first: 'The Titan, the bus for tomorrow – today.'

The major competitors to the Titan were buses designed by G.J. Rackham, who had himself been largely responsible for the Titan's chassis. In 1928 he moved to AEC and a year later the firm introduced the single-decker Regal and the double-decker Regent. Like their Leyland equivalents, they had six-cylinder engines. In 1932 AEC made a diesel engine available on all its

models and offered a Daimler pre-selector gearbox. Although 7,000 Regents were built before the war stopped production in 1942, the most famous version was the 10T10 Regal, which formed the backbone of London Transport's Green Line services in the 1930s. Their AEC 8.8-litre petrol engines had a wider power range than diesels built thirty years later.

The turn of the decade marked an enormous shift in the industry's structure. By 1930 there was a new spirit abroad, '-corporatism' – limiting competition by regulation. The 'pirate buses' of the 1920s acquired a (sometimes deserved) reputation for recklessness. The railway companies (which had been reorganized into four groups in 1923) had also moved in. 'More than anything else,' writes Hibbs[5], 'it was the appearance of the long-distance coach that hurt the railways' finances, taking

In the early 1930s, miners in the Warwickshire coalfield commuted to their work in Thornycroft buses.

away profitable traffic they could ill afford to lose.' The threat was so great that in 1928 they gained the official right to run bus services (which they'd been doing anyway – the pioneer, the Great Western Railway, had bought 100 early Milnes–Daimlers) and they started to buy into some of the biggest operators, like Thomas Tilling and British Electric Traction. In 1930 the Southern Railway bought a third stake in Southdown and formed a joint committee to consider road rail matters. They remained a major influence on bus travel until nationalization just after the war, although by the mid-1930s they had moved entirely out of bus operation.

Railway-run services were not confined to Britain, as we can see from the story of Greyhound (pages 78–81). In 1911 the mighty French railway company PLM (Paris–Lyon Méditerranée) started to run an early and ambitious service from Nice north through the French Alps to Evian. They used Berliet vehicles holding up to sixteen passengers and a vast quantity of luggage. The drivers were rigorously chosen and had to submit to a strict medical examination. In 1931 their example was followed by André Citroën, who started his own bus services using vehicles with all-steel bodies based on American Budd patents). Almost inevitably his example was soon followed by their great rival, Renault.

Within a few years both countries were firmly encased in a regulatory straitjacket which, in the case of Britain, was to last for over fifty years. The Road Traffic Act of 1931 was piloted through the House of Commons by Herbert Morrison, later deputy leader of the Labour party. But it was a non-party measure, reflecting the corporatist and protectionist ideas prevailing at the time. A lot of its provisions were belated attempts to tighten up the industry's often lax and dangerous practices and to establish the use of timetables and standard fares. But in the elaborate regulatory system the Act set up, priority was given to allocating licences to the best-established operators, and, as John Hibbs[6] puts it, 'The independent operators were never consulted, nor were the interests of consumers even given direct attention.'

The Act might have guaranteed standards – of driving, of vehicles and of services – but it was at the cost of stifling innovation and practically barring the door to newcomers. 'Had the Road Traffic Act been passed five years earlier,' observes Hibbs, 'very many coach services would not have been started.' As might have been expected, the new system provided the railways with some protection against buses by limiting the peak services of the road vehicles to three times their basic service. Yet the new regime did not prevent the decade from becoming the heyday of urban public transport in Britain, although some of it, like the replacement of trams by trolleybuses, and the extension of London's Underground, had nothing to do with buses.

The 1930s saw the consolidation of a rather muddled but effective pattern of ownership. There were the handful of major groups, like BET and Tilling, a larger number of municipally owned companies, and an even greater number of independents, mostly confined to rural areas (although many were bought up by the bigger groups). They co-existed happily enough, totally unaware of the sharp distinction that would later be drawn between private and public ownership.

By the end of the 1930s the bus and the coach between them had helped foment a revolution, especially in rural areas. As an advertisement for one operator boasted: 'Linking up villages where there are, in many cases, no longer train services, Everingham Bros AEC Regals not only provide essential transport services, but give country people a standard of travel equal to anything in the big towns.' Or, as an elderly friend of mine observed: 'Buses saved the Gloucestershire village where I live from the worst effects of the inbreeding inevitable in a small isolated rural community.'

'Co-ordination', the buzzword of the 1930s, applied also to long-distance services. It could be informal, like the famous 'two o'clock departure' at Cheltenham, the pre-motorway hub of long-distance coach services. Every day coaches would arrive between midday and 1.30pm and would leave again at 2pm. It made for an impressive sight as thousands of passengers milled around. Or the agreement could be formal, as in the case of the Limited Stop Pool of services on the Great North Road. This had started in 1928 and by the mid-1930s was responsible for a network of regular services, not just linking the north-east to London, but also providing regular two-hourly services to Liverpool and a daily service to Coventry.

(Above) A classic picture of rural Derbyshire in 1913: bus, car and motorcycle with sidecar outside The Cat and Fiddle, before the days of drink-drive legislation.

powered bus in Britain entered service with the Sheffield Corporation in March 1930. The engine was cheaper to run than a petrol-driven one – diesel was taxed less heavily than petrol and by the time the tax was equalized (by Neville Chamberlain in 1935), the diesel-engined buses were well established. In 1931 the appearance on the roads of the first Gardner LW oil engines finally established diesel motive power. Within four years a third of all the buses registered in Britain were diesel-powered.

The diesel's advantages, notably its reliability, increased pulling power and low fuel consumption, were reinforced by the use, first by Daimler and then by other manufacturers, of the Wilson pre-selector epicyclic gearbox coupled to a fluid flywheel. This allowed drivers to choose when to change gear, and greatly reduced the previous high level of skill required by a driver, who had previously had to tackle the delicate problem – particularly acute in urban areas – of using a crash box.

The 1930s also saw the introduction of what would today be called the minibus. As we have seen, the first were made by Bedford, as byproducts of the first ranges of Bedford trucks. The twenty-seat WLB introduced in 1931 (and priced competitively at £265), and the WRTB, which replaced it four years later and was fitted with a new 28hp petrol engine in late 1937, enjoyed great success – over 3,000 were built in the four years before the war. After the war Bedford introduced the OB, a development of the previous range, but then moved into larger

The 1930s were also the heyday of the touring coach, popularly known as the charabanc, which was an important element in a particular period of British social history as the annual holiday became the norm. In their day – roughly the forty years from the 1920s to the 1960s, when Britons started to look abroad and the package air tour took over the mass holiday business – charabancs were a potent symbol of communal jollity.

But the name had social connotations. The *Oxford English Dictionary* gives three definitions, 'a benched carriage', 'a kind of long and light vehicle with transverse seats looking forward' and, by extension, 'a motor coach'. Typical of the snobbery engendered by the whole idea of mass coach travel was a remark made by Ronald Knox, the well-known man of letters (and quoted as a primary source in the O.E.D.) who referred to 'charabanc-loads of buzzy Midlanders'. The word charabancs implied the invasion of beauty spots by hordes of undesirables. 'One fine day perhaps,' observed the *London Mercury*[7], 'the charabancers will awake to the fact that what they came for is no longer there.'

The remorseless advance of the bus to the detriment of the tram in towns and the railway in the country was greatly boosted by the introduction of diesel engines.** The first diesel-

(Right) The Model T Ford could be stretched to hold up to a dozen passengers.

buses with the SB, which could hold thirty-three seats. This move left operators requiring a minibus which could seat twenty to thirty people, rather bereft, so they struggled for decades in ever-increasing desperation to keep their OBs on the road in the absence of any alternative.

In the second world war buses were standardized by the Ministry of Supply, the mainstay being the Guy Arab, a much-loved if utilitarian machine. But the two decades after the end of the war saw an explosion in the numbers of bus types, encouraged at first by a similar explosion in demand from passengers and thus from operators who had run their pre-war fleets into the ground. In 1951 the 500 buses run by the Lincolnshire Road Car Company included no fewer than ninety-seven model types. And in the twenty-five years after the war Edinburgh Corporation tried out thirty-three different types. Twenty were from the Big Three, Leyland, AEC and Daimler, but there were also examples from such once-famous names as Albion, Crossley – and even Sentinel. The operators could afford to remain choosy, thus slowing down any form of rationalization.

The immediate postwar era saw the start of the sorting-out process among British manufacturers. As Gavin Booth[8] puts it:

When the Titan first appeared it was one of nine double-deck chassis on the market ... but by the mid-1950s there were really only four chassis in the race, the [AEC] Regent, the [Daimler] CV, the [Guy] Arab and the Titan.

Nevertheless, the operators were not only numerous and individualistic, they were also conservative. When Leyland introduced the Olympic with what was then a radical novelty, a monococque body, it didn't sell and they were forced to produce the Tiger, which had a 'proper', separate chassis.

Despite this setback the postwar period saw a number of important new designs. One of the most original was the Bristol Lodekka, introduced in 1949, the first bus which managed to combine a low overall height – 13ft 4ins (4.04m) – with normal seating on both decks. They achieved this with a single offset drive shaft leading to the offside of a redesigned low-centre back axle. This kept the height down without resorting to the previous expedient of having a dropped gang-

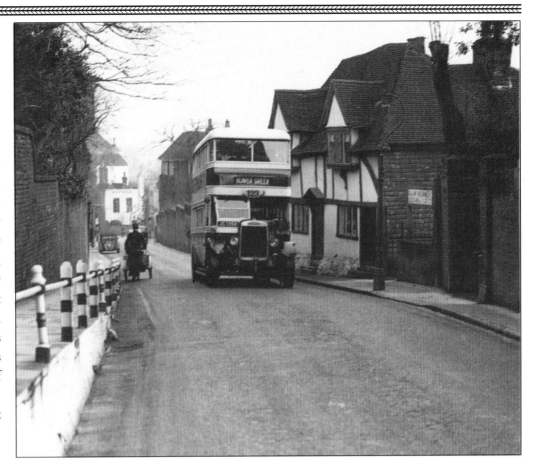

By 1939, the rural bus was a familiar sight in small towns like Ashford in Kent.

way on the top deck. With these gangways the seats were three a side, which made it very difficult for the conductors to collect the fares – though the passengers, who had never known anything different, didn't seem to care. Bristol also devised the best design for a rear-engined single-decker, with the engine driving a gearbox ahead of the rear axle.

The biggest seller, however, was Leyland's Titan PD2, which was introduced in 1947, the first of a new generation of buses with bigger engines, smoother gears and more rounded bodies. Gavin Booth[9] writes:

Looking back, the Titan arrived at just the right time when postwar loadings were reaching their peak and its bigger engine and adaptable layout guaranteed it a long and successful life, and an enviable reputation among bus operators.

Operators remained faithful to the Titan, and to other heavyweights such as the AEC Regal Mark IV, which weighed nine and a half tons, remaining dubious of the lightweight bodies used on many buses in the 1950s, even though these saved over a ton in weight and as a result gave over 10mpg (3.5kpl), while at the same time proving sturdy enough to last the twenty years expected of any bus.

Leyland, and to a certain extent AEC, were the only manufacturers to offer their own engines and were therefore not at the mercy of outside suppliers. The conservative policy of Gardner, most notably, in only slowly increasing power and production often caused problems.

Leyland introduced the Atlantean, the engine of which was placed in a flexible mounting below the floor of the back of the vehicle. This created room for an additional six seats, better comfort and a more convenient entrance, while drivers appreciated the semi-automatic gearbox. They also built the Atlantean

in coach form – the Ribble Bus Company in Preston ran a fleet of them called 'The Gay Hostesses'. Unfortunately, the engine tended to overheat because of the lack of air flow and the driver couldn't see (or smell) the problem until it was too late. More satisfactory was the Fleetline, the Gardner-engined bus introduced by Daimler in 1960, which, like the Lodekka, could go under low bridges. Both designs came into their own after one-man operation was legalized in 1966 – indeed, the Atlantean continued in production until the early 1980s. But, ironically, all these buses came into service just as demand was declining, and it took the industry another thirty years to cope with the market for flexible types of buses, including larger types of minibuses.

The great postwar boom in urban bus services – which reached its peak in 1952, when Midland Red's 2,000 buses covered seventy-five million miles in and around Birmingham – was matched by a similar demand for long-distance coach travel in a period when a general restlessness, an aching desire

In the late 1940s, the Bedford OB was the ideal vehicle for a small bus operator like Weeden's in rural Cambridgeshire.

A coach trip round the Sussex countryside, starting on Brighton sea-front, was one of the few treats available in the austerity of postwar Britain.

to escape from the prevailing austerity, was matched by an acute shortage of private cars. The operators were able to rely on a new generation of single-deckers. These had underfloor engines (a novelty pioneered, unsuccessfully, by Sentinel) and took full advantage of the increase in permitted sizes – the width limit was increased by 6ins (15cm) to 8ft (2.44m) and the length by 2½ft (76cm) to 30ft (9.14m). Such coaches could seat up to forty-one passengers, eight more than previously.

All the regional operators started their own coach services. The vehicles themselves were very different and the drivers were unlike those on a bus. They had to be polite guides and coach interiors had to be kept up to scratch – passengers could soon tell if the coach was merely a cheap conversion from a bus not a 'proper' coach. Typically, Grey–Green had a special

body made by Thomas Harrington of Hove, complete with plenty of polished walnut. It found no difficulty in keeping its fleet of 200 coaches busy every day, as well as the 300 it hired in every weekend. Between Sunday and Friday the coaches were employed on day trips, while on Saturdays they took holidaymakers off on their week's or fortnight's holiday, often to the new holiday camps on the east coast at Skegness or Clacton (they even ran special Sunday services from the east end and Stamford Hill for Jews, who were unable to travel on Saturday – often to Broadstairs where there was a synagogue).

The drivers felt that they were an elite band. One former soldier, Bill Forest, taken on because he could speak German, remembers how he worked hard but averaged £1 ($1.50) a head in tips from the usually middle-class passengers, who were far more affluent than their successors in the 1960s. He recalls that the coaches had a huge sunshine roof, wind-down windows, jelly-mould light fittings and seat covers made of soft, luxurious moquette. The tips were vital: Tom McLachlan of Grey–Green remembers receiving a fiver, more than his weekly wage, just for reserving a few seats. Indeed, some drivers relied on tips all summer and waited until the barren times of winter to take their summer wages.

The coaches penetrated far afield. By 1948 it was possible to tranship coaches to the continent (though a crane was required to lift them on and off the ferries), and at least one company was able to run 'circular tours' to the Riviera. Pure coach tours were soon supplemented by 'air–coach' tours on which the holidaymakers flew to join their coach, sometimes as far inland as Luxembourg.

In 1949 Vladimir Reitz went one step further and organized the first pure air tour, to Corsica. By the early 1960s the continental coach tour had been relegated to the third division of travel.

The same applied to buses: by the end of the 1950s they were in steady decline because of the rapid increase in car ownership, which affected coaches as well as buses, and the simultaneous rise of television. This destroyed the picture-going habit which had guaranteed a steady flow of passengers for rural operators in the evenings. And by that time full employment meant that it was becoming increasingly difficult to recruit suitable drivers, if only because of the antisocial hours worked by bus and coach drivers alike. Since then it has been downhill all the way, a decline accelerated by bus deregulation in the mid-1980s.

THE DRIVING OF BUSES IS A SERIOUS MATTER

IN 1905 A FRENCH BROCHURE 'Omnibus Automobiles',[10] was published to help would- be providers of bus services to lay down the duties expected of drivers. These were clearly an elite, and a hard-working one at that. They had to be 'sober, prudent fellows, ready to stop their vehicle when they see a frightened animal ... they should be sent to the manufacturers to learn in depth about the vehicle they are going to drive'.

Driving was not easy:

A good mechanic should slow down in towns ... and also on descents (where he should never exceed 10–12 kph [6–7.5mph]) ... .he will evade all obstacles, stones, and in towns the rubbish which

can hide pieces of broken glass which could damage the bandages [round the tyres]. If he comes across fresh gravel he should either avoid it or proceed at walking speed. In heavy rain to avoid skids he should bind a heavy rope round the rear tyres.

He was also responsible for the care of his vehicle:

The mechanic should wash his vehicle when he returns to the garage ... having carefully removed the cushions and the lights he should brush the interior with a feather duster before washing it with a powerful water jet, thoroughly clean the dirtiest corners and wash the greasy spots with a sponge and water mixed with a little paraffin, before wiping with a leather and polishing the brasswork.

He then had to fill up with water, oil and petrol, grease the wheels (without forgetting the chains) and grease the whole power train; clean the candles if need be and make sure of the brakes, the bandages and the batteries. 'Finally prepare the warning lights and the headlights, beat the carpets and the cushions ... In summer the bandages should be washed in fresh water after twenty kilometres [twelve and a half miles].'

Even at stops the driver was not off-duty: 'A good mechanic never stays on his seat when the vehicle comes to a halt; he must always have as his primary concern the care of the machine which has been put in his charge.'

In the 1930s, Tilling-Stevens both made and operated buses. This glamorous vehicle featured 'wide windows' and 'a degree of comfort hitherto associated only with first-class Pullman travel' – a direct knock at the railways.

L ONDON WAS LUCKY that the motor bus arrived when it did, in the first decade of the twentieth century. Had it been available in the 1890s it would probably have been impossible to raise the immense sums of capital required to provide London with its incomparable system of deep underground railways.

In principle there were three possible contenders for powering London's buses: petrol-electric, steam, and the internal combustion engine. And,

at the start, it was by no means easy to predict the winner, let alone that it could replace the electric tram which reached its peak of efficiency and coverage in the early years of the century.

The petrol-electric, in the form of the Tilling–Stevens engine, soon faded, hit by lack of power on London's steep and numerous slopes, but the steam engine was another matter. The major contender was the National Steam Bus, designed by Thomas Clarkson, who is described

by Maurice Kelly[11] as 'the most talented designer of steam-driven vehicles that this country has produced, manufacturing sophisticated modern vehicles when others were content to make lumbering monsters'.

In 1905 the London Road Car Company bought twenty-four of the double-decker buses Clarkson had exhibited at the Olympia fair that year. The public preferred them to the noisy, unreliable and rackety petrol-engined vehicles of the time – passengers in Clarkson's buses even enjoyed electric lighting from a small generator powered by some of the spare steam at a time when its petrol-engined rivals were fitted with oil lamps. The engine itself was a square double acting unit placed across the centre of the bus, an efficient undertype using a superheater to raise the steam pressure to 300lb/psi and the temperature to 800°F (427°C).

Clarkson never stopped innovating. As Kelly[12] says: 'He had a habit of making additions and improvements to each vehicle as he produced it.' The final result was by no means perfect, however:

> Sometimes the burners of these buses gave minor troubles when on the road; sometimes they would go out and clouds of white vaporised gas would emerge from the bonnet whilst the driver would just throw a lighted match at the grating and the burner then reignited with a loud bang ... also they blew back [which] caused an alarming display of fire beneath the bus.

In 1908 there were more Bussing buses (imported by Straker's) on the streets of London than any other type. The number 3 bus still runs through south London.

These little local difficulties, combined with the skill and endurance required of the drivers, led to the disappearance of the 'Nationals' from London streets in November 1919, and the abandonment of the whole idea of the steam bus a year later.

The Milnes–Daimler of 1904 (see page 59) was the first serious motorized contender. The opportunity it presented was eagerly seized by the fledgling London Motor Omnibus Company, which, unlike its better-established rivals, had no experience with horse buses. Originally, the LMOC used the name Vanguard, first for its routes and then for its fleet. In the following few years the numbers of motor buses operated by all three London bus companies expanded fast: from a mere twenty buses on the streets in January 1905 there were 230 by the end of that year and 800 at the end of 1906. Two years later Vanguard merged with its great rivals, General and Road Car, to form the London General Omnibus Company which from then on provided the backbone of London's bus services, although it was not until 1933 with the formation of the London Passenger Transport Board, that the concern's monopoly was finally established.

The first result of the merger was the B Type, the first truly successful mass-produced bus the world has ever seen and the first specifically designed for use in London. The Associated Equipment Company ('associated' in the sense that it had formerly been the subsidiary of an operating company) began design work in March 1910 and the bus started plying its trade on 18 October. At the end of that month an historic turning point was reached when there were exactly the same number (1,142) of motorized and horse-drawn buses on the streets of London. The B type, which featured a 30hp four-cylinder engine and a greatly improved gearbox, was the first London bus to be loved, partly because of its use during the first world war.

By 1928, Londoners were able to travel in buses which had roofs over the upper decks, but there were still plenty of the earlier open-top buses. Competition from pirates ensured regular services.

The 1920s was the decade of the bus wars in London, during which the major grouping was challenged by a number of often well-equipped '-pirates'. The first was A.G. Partridge, who pitted his Chocolate Express against LGOC on London's favourite route, the number 11. His challenge was a formidable one – his backers included Leyland. Within eighteen months there were 500 pirate buses, which were very popular with the public, on the streets of London. Often the pirates used vehicles made by Leyland and Dennis which were better than those of the LGOC. In spite of amalgamations and failures there were still fifty-four independents running 279 vehicles when the LPTB was formed in 1933.

During the 1920s the Metropolitan Police helped the operators and the designers through the gradual relaxation of some of their more absurd restrictions. In 1925 they removed the ban on covers for the upper deck, but the ban on enclosed cabs (or even windscreens) for the wretched drivers remained in place until the 1930s.

The first improvements were seen in the K Type, which replaced the B Type during the early 1920s. It was not only bigger, with forty-six seats as opposed to thirty-four in the B Type, it also eliminated the last vestiges of horse-bus design with the removal of seats running lengthwise down the bus. Its straight sides gave ample room for cross seats. The NS[1], introduced in 1923, was developed by AEC and the LGOC, and started as a solid-tyred bus restricted to 12mph (19kph). By this time, the special requirements for buses running in London were being.

Fog at 10 a.m. on a November day in 1934 turned day into night in the City of London – note the mix of buses.

Proof that the Routemaster, the last and greatest bus specially designed for conditions in London, was incredibly stable, even at an angle of over 30 degrees from the vertical.

established – for instance, six-wheelers were tried but discarded as too cumbersome for the capital's narrow and crowded streets.

By the time the LPTB was established the bus had been transformed. In the words of Barker and Robbins:[13]

The bus of 1933 was a very different thing from its predecessor only fourteen years before. In 1919 the passenger travelled on a small, solid-tyred open-top boneshaker … by 1930 the much longer, pneumatic-tyred bus with a covered top and seats upholstered throughout [had arrived].

The next thirty years brought to perfection the very special buses required to cope with conditions in the capital. They had to be nippy, with robust transmission and braking and thus able to cope with the sharp corners and the endless stopping and starting which characterized the metropolitan bus services. They had to be comfortable, to lure passengers away from taxis and private cars. They had to have an open rear platform so that Londoners could use the buses informally, hopping on and off as they pleased (proper bus stops had only been introduced between the wars – before that passengers had hailed a bus as they

would a cab). The result was a series of buses which symbolized the capital's pride in its transport system.

All the buses were, of course, powered by the oil engine. The switch was decided by the board on 6 July 1933, partly because fuel taxes had increased and the type perfected. This was not a painless process. Barker and Robbins[14] quote one engineer describing how 'the defects developed like rabbits – crankshaft bearing and timing chain life was measured in days and cylinder wear was twice that of the petrol engine, while the life of piston and ring assemblies was equally poor.'

The next standard type was the LT, which first ran in 1929 (it was the thirty-seventh type of chassis to be built for London), followed by the ST or Regent type, with a six-cylinder petrol engine. It was a forty-eight-seater – an advanced version, the ST1, had sixty seats.

In the fifteen years after the war Londoners relied on the RT Regent Mark 3[††], originally produced in January 1940. It was the first truly modern bus, the first double-decker made of metal. It had an AEC six-cylinder 9.6-litre oil engine, with a fluid flywheel and preselector gearbox. The body was even more special: the structure underneath was carefully concealed, every screw and bolt hidden and every angle rounded. Every detail, from the window winders to the abstract pattern of the upholstery, had been carefully thought through – even the driver, usually neglected, had a fully adjustable seat.

But the final triumph of the type was the Routemaster, undoubtedly the finest vehicle ever designed for public transport anywhere in the world and still in use nearly forty years after it was first introduced. In the words of Jonathan Glancey:[15] 'It was to be up-to-the-minute but not gimmicky. It was therefore built as a sophisticated kit of parts that could be taken apart, renewed and put together again without too many problems.' It had independent suspension, power steering, a fully automatic gear change, a proper heating system and a far more comfortable cab for the driver.

Yet the Routemaster was not the result of revolutionary design, but of endless painstaking improvements on even the tiniest aspects of bus construction. For example, the way it was curved throughout meant there were no dirt traps. After four years' development work the final version, powered by an AEC 9.6-litre direct-injection engine, went into service in 1958.

Unfortunately the tradition was broken in 1968 when the then Labour government decided that standard buses could service London just as well as LT's own design. Of course, they couldn't stand up to the conditions, notably the constant stopping and starting, and the consequent strain imposed on the brakes, the transmission and the cooling system. In spite of this, the decision meant the end of the special type of bus which Londoners had loved for the previous sixty years.

THE STORY OF GREYHOUND BUSES reflects both the social and economic history of twentieth-century America, combining as it does the rise and fall of the country's thousands of small towns, the excitement of the early motor age, the decline in group travel, and of inner cities, and, not least, the triumph of the private car and the short-hop airline.

The firm's founder was Carl Eric Wickman, a young Swedish immigrant who received his initiation in the mining camps of Minnesota. The training was rough: as a friend remarked, he 'never saw him duck a fight or lose one'.[16] He started his business in 1913 largely by default: he had the local Hupmobile dealership but couldn't sell any of the vehicles, so he used one of these impressive seven-seaters to transport his fellow miners to the fleshpots of a nearby town called Alice.

He quickly expanded, building up a fleet of eighteen cars, but even in these early years he was thinking on a national level, working through an increasingly elaborate network of affiliates as well as direct subsidiaries. He ultimately played a central role in disciplining many of the country's 6,500 independent bus operators, insisting on interchangeable tickets and mass purchasing to counter the power of the bus manufacturers.

He became such an important customer that General Motors stepped in to save him by taking on some of his by then excessive debts when the depression struck in 1929–30. He was also greatly helped by his enemies, the railroad companies. In 1928 the Great Northern had bought 80 percent of his company, Northland, while allowing him (and his firm) to expand elsewhere. It was the subsequent absorption of other lines, including a larger rival, the Yelloway system, which transformed Wickman's company into Greyhound – a name coined, it is said, by an onlooker watching an early Fageol bus sweep past.

During the 1930s the railroads helped even more by lapping up the stocks and bonds issued by Greyhound to finance its acquisition surge. By 1933, the Greyhound corporation included fourteen major subsidiaries or affiliates ranging from Pennsylvania to the south. Even the increasing regulation by the Interstate Commerce Commission did not prevent Greyhound from expanding, although the ICC did stop some acquisitions.

Greyhound's greatest days were probably the late 1930s, when its fame was created by a fair and a film. The fair was in Chicago in 1933. Greyhound seized their opportunity by offering all-expenses-paid tours from every state in the country. The film It Happened One Night, was the winner of numerous Oscars in 1934. Much of the action of Frank Capra's romantic comedy took place on a bus, and seeing Clark Gable and Claudette Colbert on an Atlantic Greyhound bus removed the previous stain of tackiness associated with the new form of travel.

By then Greyhound, which owned nearly 1,700 buses, was strong enough to compete with the railroads, and its buses were world leaders made by General Motors. Greyhound had no central research – its engineers were scattered throughout the country so that they were available to tend to the needs of local drivers and passengers. In its heyday, the quarter of a century after 1933, Greyhound could legitimately boast a long list of

Greyhound's postwar buses were not only good-looking, they were also a convincing symbol of contemporary American engineering pride.

firsts: the use of diesel engines, an all-diesel fleet, rear engines, turbo-chargers, automatic transmissions, air suspension, air conditioning, central heating, power steering (introduced in an experimental coach as early as 1946), and specifying the installation of lavatories on all new coaches.

The first bus to fulfil Wickman's dreams was the streamlined Supercoach developed by General Motors and styled by Raymond Loewe, which Greyhound introduced in 1936. Advertised, not without reason, as 'the most beautiful and spacious motor coach yet conceived', it still looks elegant and modern nearly sixty years later. Wickman also developed bus terminals which, like the underground stations and bus garages London Transport was building in the same period, are still splendid examples of bold, simple, modern architecture.

After the war the surge continued. By 1949 Greyhound was promoting 'Amazing America Tours' on some of its fleet of 5,837 coaches. It was also experimenting with a new fifty-seater called the Highway Traveler powered by two air-cooled motors developed by Greyhound's own engineers. The coach was a two-level affair, boasting a lavatory, refrigerators, three air-conditioned compartments and air suspension. It fully justified the advertisement 'Go Greyhound and leave the driving to us.'

Greyhound bought 500 at a cost of $220 million (£146.7 million) from GM to meet the post-war surge in demand. By 1951 it had 6,280 buses providing services along nearly 90,000 miles of highway. In 1954 it introduced the Scenicruiser which had an observation deck, in time to run on the rapidly expanding network of interstate highways.

One of the major sources of Greyhound's supremacy in the 1930s: the much-trumpeted service it provided for visitors to Chicago's 1933 World Fair.

Bus stations like this one at Evansville, Indiana, were symbols of the glamour of bus travel in the 1930s. The same simplicity and elegance can be found in the bus garages built for London Transport at the time.

In retrospect, this can be seen as the high point of the Greyhound story. There were strikes and mechanical problems with the new coach, compounded by terrible organizational traumas as the veterans who had founded the company with Wickman, who were by this time ageing and quarrelsome, started to retire.

From then on the story became corporate as well as social, as new managers diversified a company whose strength had been its singleness of purpose, trying to avoid the decline, in status even more than traffic, engendered by the post-war rise of short-haul air travel, and the decay of the inner cities where the Greyhound bus station had formerly been such a star attraction.

* Of De Dion-Bouton fame. Buses designed by De Dion, and its German rivals, Daimler and Bussing, were also used by early British bus operators, notably
  in London – the vehicles were sold as Straker–Squires, the Daimler as Milnes–Daimler.
** Often called 'oil engines' at the time. For many years the description 'diesel' was shunned by the purists.
† The name had a number of possible origins: Nulli Secundus, or New S type, or it could refer to the fact that the vehicle had No Step.
†† The exact meaning and origin of the term RT has been a matter of almost theological debate for nearly half a century.

Chapter Five

YOU'RE IN THE ARMY NOW

ONVENTIONAL HISTORY has it that the second world war was the first mechanized war, the first dominated by motorized transport. This is untrue on two counts: the German army, the first to introduce motorized warfare, in fact relied to an enormous extent on horse-drawn transport throughout the second world war; moreover, the history of motorized transport in warfare goes back to the Crimean war. Since then its role has grown steadily but implacably.

By 1939 vehicles of all kinds were being used for every type of military duty. But their relationship with normal civilian transport varied wildly. A staff car or light van was merely a civilian vehicle in khaki: at the other end of the scale, no one had much use for a battle tank outside its military context. What is interesting is the relationship between civilian and military, how developments in motorized transport for both purposes influenced each other.

'War transforms haulage', as the saying has it. Even in wars fought largely by foot soldiers their baggage and their supporting artillery required heavy transport, 'baggage trains'. Even before the French revolution Captain Nicolas Joseph Cugnot had mounted a steam boiler on a three-wheel carriage to act as an artillery tractor.° Although the contraption reached 3mph (5kph) the steering went awry and the gallant Captain was jailed for his pains.

But the lesson had been learned, at least by one key figure. In 1797 the paper submitted by one Napoleon Bonaparte to support his membership of the Institut Français was entitled 'The automobile in war', though in his time the steam engine was not sufficiently widely available to prove his point.

By the mid-nineteenth century the growth of railways led to the assumption that steam power could be applied to the problem of military haulage. A Boydell steam-powered traction engine was used in the Crimean war between 1854 and 1856 after special footed wheels had been fitted to cope with the muddy conditions. From then on their use gradually spread. In 1870–71 the Prussian army used Fowler engines to haul artillery during the Franco–Prussian war. In 1870 a young British engineer officer, Lt R.E. Crompton, conducted a series of experiments with road steamers in both Britain and India. By 1873 Steam Sappers were ordered by the Royal Engineers from Aveling & Porter. The engines weighed only five tons; the 6hp they produced from a conventional locomotive-type boiler was enough to tow a fifteen-ton train over rough country, including that encountered during the Ashanti war over the next couple of years.

It was John Fowler of Leeds who continued to dominate the scene. In 1879 a British test of a Fowler artillery siege train reported that it:

(Opposite) In 1917 the Scottish Fusiliers still had some horse-drawn vehicles, but most of those rumbling over the cobbled streets of Poperinge were Mack Bulldogs.

hauled a train of no less than fourteen field guns (total weight thirty-four tons [34.5 tonnes]) over roads, fields and marsh at an average speed of 4mph (6kph). The performance of the siege train engine was no less impressive in marshy conditions. It towed a forty- pounder gun (weighing four tons) across boggy ground until the entire equipage was completely stuck to its axles and immobilized in the mud...Using a wire rope and the powered capstan, the vehicle hauled itself free after the rope had been passed round a suitable tree. Then it ... proceeded on its journey.[1]

In the Boer war at the turn of the century, Crompton, by now a colonel, adapted some MacLaren 70hp standard Colonial engines used in the diamond fields. They were compound engines, with both high- and low-pressure cylinders, and had the advantage of extra water tanks and especially large grates for burning wood. The British army even armoured some of their steam road trains but they were terribly slow.

The first real impact of armies on the world's infant motor industries came in the run-up to the first world war, with schemes to provide what were called 'subsidy trucks', designed to provide the military with a stock of suitable vehicles when

Naval interest in mechanized gun tractors: the Churchillian figure of Admiral Bacon watching trials of the Foster–Daimler tractor.

A convoy of Mack Bulldogs taking British troops for a rest after the battle of Guillemont, in September 1916.

hostilities began. The result benefited both the military and the fledgling motor manufacturers.

The Germans provided subsidies for what they termed 'Leichter Armee Lastzug'. This definition covered 'light military vehicles', a range of vehicles which included a four-ton truck and a two-ton four-wheel-drive tractor. The regulations were strict – six-ton tractors had to work in wintry conditions, they had to be easy to repair and to cope with a variety of fuels. The need for such trucks was shown in 1914 when three quarters of the 64,000 motor vehicles in use in Germany were mobilized.

In 1911 the British had started a more modest programme covering a mere 1,000 vehicles. In return for keeping trucks available for military use manufacturers received a £30 ($45) enrolment fee and a further £80 ($120) in six half-yearly instalments for three-ton and 30-cwt (1,524-kg) vehicles – by 1914 the war office had only eighty vehicles of its own, the rest of the fleet (amounting by this time to nearly 1,200 in all) were 'subsidy' vehicles made by a select group of manufacturers, including Dennis, Maudslay, Hallford, Karrier, Leyland, Thornycroft and Wolseley. The Thornycroft J Type proved a

The Thornycroft 'J' Type, with its four-cylinder 40bhp side-valve engine was one of the most successful products of the 'subsidy' scheme which supported many countries' vehicle industries.

particular success with its four-cylinder side-valve engine which developed 40hp. The trucks were used as mobile workshops and as mounts for anti-aircraft guns.

From 1909, the Automobile Club de France organized tests on behalf of the Ministry of War. In a scheme similar to the British one, every purchaser of every vehicle chosen had to guarantee to keep it in good repair. In return he received four annual bonuses. By 1913 twenty types had been chosen and the tests greatly accelerated the introduction of technical innovations like roller bearings, improved brakes, and much better rubber bandages round the wheels replacing iron bindings. As a result, the French found themselves with 6,000 trucks on the outbreak of war

The French also showed the greatest technical ingenuity. No fewer than eleven vehicles developed specifically for military use were on view at the Universal Exposition in Paris in 1900.

These included:

a De Dion–Bouton Tricar for liaison work, Decauville and Mors staff cars, a Panhard and Levassor bus adapted as a troop transport, a De Dietrich medical van, a Sautter telegraph wagon and van, a pigeon van, a military post office van, a Sotte [steam] tractor, and, finally, a De Dion–Bouton steam lorry.[2]

French ingenuity also resulted in the Ravaillier amphibious car of 1910 which had a wooden, boat-shaped body and a propeller driven from the rear-mounted engine. It looked odd but could reach 20mph (32kph) on land and 9mph (14.5kph) in the water, complete with a two-rope windlass, oars and foghorn.

The various vehicles being produced across Europe had to compete in some extraordinary tests. The most extreme consisted of a 25,000km (15,534-mile) drive around Russia, which involved many hazards (one Swiss Saurer truck was attacked by a horde of drunken peasants). The tests showed the advances made by the Germans, most notably by Mercedes, with a vehicle which had moulded steel wheels, and by Benz, whose engines had double ignitions in each cylinder, one from a magneto, the other from an accumulator.

In contrast to the Europeans, the Americans, lacking the impetus generated in Europe by the tensions which were to lead to war, were slow off the mark, although one vehicle, a 20hp Hupmobile Runabout, bought by the military in 1911, became famous as a scout car. For years they merely dabbled, despite an official report which stated firmly that trucks could 'handle all road conditions – sandy, dry, very wet and heavily rutted'.[3]

Then, in 1912, vehicles made by FWD, White and Autocar travelled 1,500 miles (2,414km) through the south in forty-five days, averaging thirty-three miles (fifty-three kilometres) per day (and once covering 112 miles [180km]), far faster than the pack mules previously used, despite atrocious conditions including one stretch in which a horse had been drowned in a hole in the road.

Although the Allied armies had already started to order American trucks, especially the Mack Bulldog, in large numbers, it was the punitive expedition in Mexico led by General Pershing in 1916 which made the point most effectively. The Americans couldn't use the railways because of Mexican political sensibilities. But the 588 vehicles of thirteen different makes they used performed so well in 'the hardest test of motor truck transportation they had ever known' that the military started to order in quantity.

In Mexico the vehicles were not used only for supply. In May 1916 one Lt George S. Patton, later to become famous as a great tank commander, conducted the first motorized assault in history when he led fifteen men in three automobiles to attack a ranch house in which one of the key aides of Pancho

The Mack Bulldog was big enough and tough enough to be able to transport the Renault FT17, one of France's first tanks.

Villa, the Mexican revolutionary, was sheltering. Patton had understood the way motorized transport could solve the problem posed by the great strategist Captain Basil Liddell Hart, that the soldier 'could not move if he wished to fire and could not fire if he wished for cover'.

But neither Liddell Hart nor Patton was the first to grasp the point. In the 1860s James Cowen, best known as a wealthy British philanthropist, had come up with the idea of an armoured traction engine with a turtle-shaped hull fitted with four light cannon. But this precursor of the tank was rejected by Lord Palmerston, the Prime Minister of the day (generally reckoned to be a bellicose and unsentimental figure) because the contraption also featured scythes fitted to the wheels, which even he found too barbaric for use in civilized warfare.

The idea was taken up by a German officer Lt-Col von Layriz. In a book entitled *Mechanical Traction at War,* published as early as 1900, he suggested mounting quick-firing guns to steam vehicles. In the first years of the century there were a number of other initiatives aimed at adapting civilian vehicles for fighting purposes. In 1902 Charron's fitted an open steel turret

over the rear axle of an ordinary passenger car. The next year, Daimler built the first armoured car with a Maxim machine-gun mounted on the chassis of a 35hp engine. This vehicle, which was capable of doing 35mph (56kph), was used by the then mighty army of the Austro–Hungarian Empire on manoeuvres.

In 1906 the Erhardt balloon destroyer was mounted on either a normal tourer body or an armoured body while in 1909 Daimler supplied a four-wheel drive truck armed with an anti-airship gun to Portuguese West Africa. That same year, the Americans tried out the first motorized gun and by 1914 the German army was using cars, complete with improvised mounts for machine-guns, for transporting its crack 'Jaeger' battalions (which saw action notably in Romania in 1916).

Winston Churchill, then First Lord of the Admiralty, saw the potential of using motorized transport for providing troops with mobile firepower after London buses had been used to transport marines sent to protect the channel ports. After they had proved their worth, Churchill's assistant, Commander Suter, commandeered every Rolls-Royce in Britain for military use and the marque became a familiar sight in the Near East, where it was

The Rolls-Royce Ghost at Aqaba, in the 'Desert War' which starred Colonel T.E. Lawrence.

The Taxis, and buses, which rushed reinforcements from Paris to the Battle of the Marne – only a few miles east of EuroDisney – in September 1914.

used by Lawrence of Arabia and General Allenby, amongst others, on the only battlefield where mobility mattered. The major competition was provided by Lanchester, a pioneering Birmingham-based company. The Lanchester, complete with epicyclic transmission, advanced suspension (double cantilever rear springs with coil springs on the front) and a six-cylinder 38hp engine, formed the basis for ambulances and for the vehicles used by the armoured car division** of the Royal Naval Air Service, another of Churchill's innovations.

Yet armoured cars were a minor aspect of motorized transport in the first world war. The bulk of transport needs were filled by hastily improvised lash-ups. The most spectacular were the Paris taxis used to rush reinforcements to the Battle of the Marne in early September 1914. The idea came from General Gallieni, the military commander in Paris, who commandeered 1,200 of the capital's fleet of 10,000 taxis to speed two regiments of infantry to the front line, a mere thirty-two miles (51.5k) east of Paris at Nanteuil. In the words of Captain C.R. Kutz:[4]

> the convoy discipline was excellent considering the eccentricities of Paris taxi drivers and the breakdowns were remarkably few. From this small beginning grew the very efficient motor transport service used by the French throughout the war. This included such specialities as the Boulant mobile surgeries built on to the chassis of Paris buses which had a 40hp engine, a top speed of 30kph (19mph), solid rubber tyres and twin rear wheels. Some of the ingenious steam engines made by Valentin Purrey were used by the French army for providing showers and disinfecting troops. The army also used some of the water trucks normally employed to clean the smarter boulevards of Paris to bring fresh drinking water to front-line troops.

CLASSIC TRUCKS

The British equivalent of the 'Taxis de la Marne' was 'Ole Bill', the B Type London bus, now proudly on display at the Imperial War Museum, one of the many used to carry British troops to the front.

These were all, essentially, adaptations of civilian vehicles for military purposes. But, as Brian Baxter[5] points out, many of them were advances on the design of civilian vehicles:

Four-wheel drive, the use of shaft drive instead of chain drive, wider use of pneumatic tyres even on three-ton lorries and the use of Caterpillar tracks all brought closer the concept of a fully mechanized army where vehicles would no longer depend on roads.

In the first world war the military had a particular influence on two major technical advances, the half-track and the four-wheel drive.

(Right) The Second Battalion of the Royal Warwickshire Regiment moving to the front in November 1914, in a convoy of B-Type buses.

(Below) Ole Bill, most famous of London B-Type buses – the symbol of the mobilization of Britain during the first world war.

The half-track evolved into both a fully tracked vehicle which just happened to have wheels in front, or a four-wheeled vehicle in which the rear wheels were replaced by tracks. As far back as the 1890s Benjamin Holt had made practical crawler tractors, or Caterpillars, as he called them. He joined forces with Daniel Best in 1908. Best's son, Clarence, founded his own firm, but merged with his father's old company to form the appropriately named Caterpillar company. Meanwhile, the French had produced an experimental vehicle, the Lefèbvre tractor, based on the Holt–Caterpillar principles, which could run either on wheels on roads or on half-tracks in rougher conditions.

The ability of Caterpillars to cross the harshest of terrain naturally appealed to the military. In 1907 the Royal Army Service Corps bought a Holt–Akroyd paraffin-engined tractor to haul heavy guns and converted it to run on Holt–Caterpillar tracks. It was a modern machine – it even had brakes actuated by compressed air.

These tracks, however, were metallic and could travel only at walking pace. Much better were the trucks equipped with the system of continuous rubber track mounted on light bogies devised by one Adolphe Kegresse, a Frenchman who was in charge of the garage of Tsar Nicholas II. These trucks proved suitable not only for bad roads but also for snow. The first trials were conducted on the Rolls-Royces and Packards in the imperial garage but 200 Kegresse-type vehicles were also produced for the Russian army.

These machines survived until 1920, when the French, fighting alongside the Poles, found themselves confronted by the Kegresses, equipped with machine-guns, in the hands of the opposing Red army. Even more extraordinary survivors were the light Ford trucks manufactured under licence in Russia in the early 1930s, which ended up in France in 1939 carrying soldiers from the defeated Spanish republican army.

Adolphe Kegresse returned to France, where André Citroën eagerly took up the idea of half-tracks, and used 'Citroën–Kegresses' in his famous long journeys, the 'Croisières', including the legendary *Croisière Jaune* from Beirut to Peking. But their services were not limited to spectacular stunts, and they found a variety of civilian uses, although the French army remained their best customer, especially during the period between 1927 and 1933 when the army was being mechanized. Although production stopped when Citroën went broke in 1934, the Austrian postal service was using them as late as 1948. The British army also had a number of Crossley and Burford lorries converted to gun- and load-carriers, using the Citroën–Kegresse tracks after they had given a spectacular performance when laying telephone cables across the country on manoeuvres in 1925.

The Kegresse idea survived as the basis for most subsequent half-tracks. These were very largely military, though they also

A Holt tractor showing how invaluable half-tracked vehicles could be in towing guns (in this case a 6-inch howitzer) and its crew.

The most practical of early half-tracks were those developed by Adolphe Kegresse, originally for the Tsar of Russia and here used on Citroën-Kegresse-HInstin armoured cars.

solved the problems created by the primitive tyres then in use – wheels were bound with a metal ring with rubber bandages around them. These wore out all too easily and posed major problems of grip.

Probably the first on the scene in this area was the French firm of Latil. (In this, as in many other developments in the industry, new ideas were being pursued simultaneously in several countries, so imprecision is the order of the day.) As early as 1898 it had started making front-wheel drive units that could replace the front axle and turntable of horse-drawn vehicles. Latil went on to add power – and sometimes steering as well – to the rear axles, and four- or five-speed gearboxes. The result proved very useful for the French army, which bought over 4,000 to use as gun tractors during the first world war.

Latil was followed by a number of other French manufacturers in producing four-wheel drive, but in the end the winners in the race for this valuable sector of the market were the Americans (although the Latil machines were so advanced that they were used by the American Expeditionary Force). The Jeffery (renamed the Nash–Quad in 1917 as a result of a take-over) closely resembled the Latil because it had four-wheel steering as well as four-wheel power.

The first American four-wheel drive was probably one made in 1904 by Couple–Gear, a vehicle with an electric motor on each wheel powered by a generator. But the most successful formula was pioneered a couple of years later by the appropriately named Four Wheeled Drive company. Its FWDs had steering and were powered on all four wheels.

Four years later, Mercedes produced a four-wheel drive, as did Skoda and Daimler (the latter used for mounting anti-airship guns). During the war, Austro–Daimler benefited from army orders for its early four-wheel drive vehicles, which gave rise to another innovation: a road train developed to haul ammunition wagons, powered by a six-cylinder engine that developed the then enormous power of 100bhp.

But the standard had been set in 1912 by FWD with its B model, a three-tonner with a four-cylinder motor producing 56bhp, which was housed under the driver's seat. It sold slowly at first and the firm was saved from failure only by the outbreak of war.

proved ideal for large snowmobiles. Yet, their later civilian use was limited: there were enough left over after the war to negate commercial prospects and the development of the pneumatic tyre enabled trucks equipped with the new low-pressure, large-section tyres to tackle conditions which had previously required half-tracks.

The half-track was used again in the second world war and not only on specially designed vehicles: it was found, for instance, that Scammell heavy breakdown tractors could easily and profitably be fitted with half-tracks and after the war old AEC Matadors with a half-track on the front were adapted for use as mobile cranes. In the 1950s Tunick Brothers in Stamford, Connecticut converted quite a lot of half-tracks into dump trucks.

More generally successful was four-wheel drive, an innovation based on strict commercial criteria. In the early part of the century four-wheel drive was essential in the United States except in a few large cities, as can be seen in the story of Oshkosh (page 128). Four-wheel drive, like half-tracks, also

The first world war had transformed the whole world transport scene by making motorized transport the norm throughout the developed world. This progress was boosted during the immediate postwar period by the enormous number of surplus vehicles left behind, most obviously by the American armies in Europe because of a natural desire not to flood their home market with them.

These trucks were largely spartan vehicles, with four-cylinder engines, shaft drives and left-hand drive, then a novelty in France. Although the Whites apparently suffered engine problems and the Packards had dodgy rear axles, others, most obviously the Mack Bulldog, set standards which the local manufacturers had to match, a rough but effective form of technical imperialism which would have proved helpful to the British, who remained over protected from advanced foreign ideas until the 1960s. At home, the US military also turned over to state highway departments hundreds of half-track ten-tonners built to haul guns or howitzers.

These trucks served as a major educational tool, bringing cheap motorized transportation to businesses hitherto too small or too remote to consider such a bold step, and thus creating whole new classes of long-term customers. Nevertheless, they undoubtedly caused serious short-term problems for the manufacturers. Typically, Marius Berliet lost control of his company for nearly a decade, and the British surplus ruined Commer, which had built 3,000 four-ton lorries during the first world war. But in Britain the most important inheritance from the war was the thousands of small, modern buses made by Chevrolet, Fiat and half a dozen other manufacturers which enabled hundreds of small operators to get a start in commercial life against larger competitors encumbered with more expensive (and cumbersome) British-made vehicles.

Even non-combatants were affected. At the end of the war the Swiss army put its surplus lorries at the disposal of the postal service which used those made by Saurer on Alpine routes and the Bernas on flatter routes.

Wars could, of course, help as well as ruin manufacturers. Leyland is a typical case. During the first world war the company produced over 6,000 vehicles for the armed forces. After the war it bought back and rebuilt many of them in a successful attempt to safeguard its good name, but the effort brought the company to its knees. By contrast, after the second world war it adapted its tank engines into the 7.4-litre E181 engine, and during the Korean war the military paid for a new factory to build tanks, a facility which proved immensely important in three subsequent decades.

In peacetime, the relationship between the motor industry and the defence establishment changes. Armed forces are no longer able to dictate their own requirements: they are short of cash, they have to wheel and deal to obtain what they want, playing second fiddle to commercial customers. This is not a new phenomenon. Before the first world war the US Army Signal Corps could not find a manufacturer willing to adapt one of its vehicles: it was simply not worth it, for there was no budget for a production run. As one manufacturer put it, they wouldn't build 'a special vehicle for possible orders for a fixed sum'.[6] The military was reduced to asking makers to build prototypes of machines which would only be ordered in bulk when war came.

The British were equally helpless. The army looked for manufacturers who would accept the idea of the military providing design specifications, testing prototypes and only then placing orders (an arrangement under which Guy, for one, flourished by designing vehicles to the army's requirements). But the reliance on civilian expertise remained strong: a manual issued by the war office in 1937 gave an elaborate description of the self-help techniques to be used with heavy vehicles in case of breakdown, ending with the recommendation that, when in doubt, drivers should use the 'local blacksmith'. As Brian Baxter[7] points out: 'They were destined to find few village blacksmiths in the deserts of north Africa.'

This resulted in adaptations: until the second world war, the British army relied on a 4-wheel 15cwt (762kg) truck without a turret, intended purely for reconnaissance purposes. As the war progressed, it was replaced by the purpose-built Daimler scout car and Bren carrier.

But even before the war the technical traffic was not only one way. Basic commercial six-tonners were improved by a new rear bogie designed by the war office, with two springs fixed above and below a central pivot and a low-pressure cross-country tyre. Later, a sand tyre was the result of joint military–civilian development. On the other side of the equation, Guy, which had switched almost completely to military production in 1936, pioneered the use of welded armoured steel, a process the firm presented to the war office free of charge. Nevertheless, an attempt to revive the pre-war subsidy scheme didn't work because civilian and military requirements had already started to diverge too widely.

By the outbreak of the second world war the military had a pretty clear idea of their (very varied) requirements. The British divided them into three categories: 'A' vehicles – armoured fighting vehicles, bearing little or no relation to ordinary commercial vehicles; the 'B' class covered vehicles used for transport, mainly lorries (a comprehensive term applied to

any vehicle which had a payload over 15cwt (762kg) – these were largely based on commercial vehicles; by contrast, the 'C' category covered all the specials, from the DUKWs used to carry troops across rivers to the vehicles adapted for use by chaplains as mobile churches.

The 'B' group included a host of legendary vehicles, from the 'Tilly' (the 10hp van mass-produced by Morris, Austin and Hillman) to the Bedford 15cwt (762kg), first built to compete in a war office trial in 1935. Although the first order was for a modest 2,000, the 15cwt accounted for most of the 250,000 vehicles produced by Bedford during the war and was used for every sort of purpose from gun-carrier to mobile tea car. But even the standard ten-ton trucks made by Albion and Leyland were based on prewar models.

The Morris 15cwt, one of the mainstays of the British war effort in the second world war.

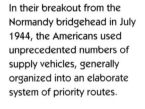

In their breakout from the Normandy bridgehead in July 1944, the Americans used unprecedented numbers of supply vehicles, generally organized into an elaborate system of priority routes.

AEC, in particular, began to build a wide range of trucks after it had absorbed the British subsidiary of the American FWD. The legendary Matador first appeared in 1939 as a gun tractor with a six-cylinder, 7.58-litre AEC engine giving 95bhp and a top speed of 36mph (58kph). A winch with 250ft (76m) of wire rope inside the chassis members allowed it to tow up to six and a half tons. The army ordered 8,600, the air force a further 400. Nonetheless, production built up so slowly that for a long time the 8th Army in Egypt relied on the sturdy Mack ten-ton 6x4 NR while it waited for newer British trucks.

The most memorable adaptations were the super-heavies. The unquestioned leader was Scammell, with its famous Pioneer (see page 132), which proved able to cope with the heaviest of jobs, transporting tanks and recovering them from the battlefield. The British army, which only had one tank transporter at the outbreak of war, also used the Diamond T wrecker employed by the Americans, which was also based on a commercial vehicle, and superheavy wreckers based on the Kenworth.

The Germans, meanwhile, had given themselves an early start. In 1938 one General Schell instituted a rationalization programme. He eliminated the majority of the sprawling range of vehicles ordered by the army up to that point and replaced them with a handful of standard designs. These included a medium truck first made by Henschel, but also built by Magirus, a most advanced design with a 100hp six-cylinder diesel engine, a five-speed gearbox and air brakes. But perhaps the most famous was the Opel Blitz a 4x2 three-tonner with a 3.6-litre six-cylinder engine developing 75bhp linked to a five-speed box – a vehicle built in over 100 variants. In addition, the Germans were able to rely for a long time on the thousands of vehicles they had captured in their conquests of much of western Europe.

The biggest manufacturers were the Americans. By the end of the second world war they had produced over three million trucks of every possible description, or one vehicle to every four men under arms, while Canada, overshadowed by its neighbour as so often, produced a further 800,000. The majority of these vehicles were of directly commercial origin and the dominant class was the two and a half-ton 6x6, the biggest truck that could be built on car-type assembly lines. By 1945 800,000 had been produced, over two thirds by General Motors – hence the nickname Jimmy (an alternative name was the Deuce and a Half).

Only such mass production could provide enough vehicles to mount ambitious exercises like the Red Ball Express, a system of priority routes from Cherbourg to the ever-more distant

The Jeep could be relied on in any circumstances, even on the rutted roads found in France in the winter of 1944–45.

The Heavy Expanded Mobility Tactical Trucks – HEMTTs for short – made by Oshkosh won praise even from 'Stormin' Norman' Schwarzkopf in the Gulf War.

front line in France. This used Macks and Whites in the world's most ambitious attempt to transport the needs of a modern army over hundreds of miles – though even the Red Ball could not, in the end, keep pace with the American advance.

Obviously, there was a vast park of vehicles available after the war, but postwar reconstruction led to such a worldwide shortage that they did not represent the same threat to the manufacturers as they had after the 1914–18 war. Even so, Dutch hauliers took such good advantage of the golden opportunity provided by the enormous dumps of surplus equipment left behind by the Americans that they captured two fifths of the international road haulage business in western Europe.

Some individual types formed the basis of postwar success. Scammell thrived, while in Germany the Opel Blitz continued in production and, as the S Type, became a mainstay of German commercial transport after the war. And, of course, war surplus vehicles were adapted by many ingenious buyers. For several decades AEC Matadors were used as maids of all work for contractors or as recovery vehicles at service stations, while Wynns used American tank transporters in their challenge to Pickfords in the field of heavy haulage. Veteran Morris 4x4 quads, originally designed to tow guns, came into their own for an equally long time as recovery vehicles or snowploughs.

Since the second world war, military vehicles have diverged more and more widely from their civilian equivalents, with obvious exceptions like the trucks used to tow aircraft or the specialized fire engines used in civilian, as in military, airports. Otherwise, the thousands of vehicles which swarmed through the Iraqi desert in early 1991 bore little resemblance to their civilian counterparts. Specialization had taken its toll of the once-fruitful interaction between the two.

* The 'truck' built by Cugnot in 1771 is generally considered to have been the first motorized vehicle.
** The use of the term 'car' rather than 'tank' shows the relationship to normal civilian vehicles. This was a purely military development.

THE LOVED ONE

THE IDEA THAT a military vehicle can be loved should be, on the face of it, ridiculous. But the fact remains that this curious machine was genuinely loved by most of those who used it. Yet, in military parlance, it was merely the most successful version of a breed born with the century: a small 4x4 vehicle capable of transporting four men and a machine-gun across the roughest country. Industrially, the Jeep is a curiosity, a survivor of second-world-war engineering (and mass production) which still flourishes in much the same form as when it first became famous fifty years ago.

But there is something about the Jeep which enabled it to transcend strict objective language. The cartoon (right) showing a distressed sergeant putting down his beloved vehicle is not ridiculous, merely an exaggeration of reality. The vehicle's attractions were summed up by Ernie Pyle, the greatest of American war correspondents (if only because he was by far the closest to the feelings of the ordinary GI):

> I do not think we could continue the war without the Jeep. It does everything. It goes everywhere. It's as faithful as a dog as strong as a mule and as agile as a goat. All the time it carries loads twice as heavy as those it was designed for and it keeps going just the same … the Jeep is a divine instrument of military locomotion.[8]

It was not only its reliability, ubiquity and its toughness which appealed, but also its crucial accessibility; the fact that, unlike any other military vehicle before or since, you could hop, slide or slither in and out as casually as you do into your trousers. It was almost an extension of your body.

Back to military basics. The Jeep was the final product of a long period of evolution. Its genesis goes back to 1904, when Captain Gentil of the

Vincennes workshops near Paris converted a Panhard to carry a Hotchkiss machine-gun. In 1912, Major Thomas Dickson of the US army did the same with a Hupmobile.

Mobility was not much in demand during the first world war, and in the interwar period the world's armies had to make do and mend. The Model T was the first of many commercially available small vehicles to be adapted for military use. It was followed by many others. The Italians relied on Fiat's Balilla Spider, partly because it was the most popular vehicle in the country and so would be available in wartime in large numbers, while at the outbreak of the second world war the French army requisitioned large numbers

of an even smaller vehicle, the Simca 5, made by Fiat's French subsidiary.

The German army turned down the otherwise successful Tempo, made by Vidal und Söhn, which boasted two two-cylinder engines, and instead took the basic floorpan and suspension of the Volkswagen, the 'People's Car' which Dr Porsche had designed for mass production in the 1930s, and adapted it as the Kubelwagen. This proved extremely handy, offering a performance which nearly matched that of a four-wheel drive vehicle. In the course of the war 52,000 were built and put into service to carry every type of load – troops, munitions and fuel – and were used by engineers and as ambulances. The Kubelwagen

In 1970 the Jeep Corporation celebrated the 30th anniversary of a vehicle so beloved that it broke a solider's heart to get rid of it – cartoonist Bill Mauldin was not exaggerating.

The German Kubelwagen, derived from the early Volkswagen, proved invaluable to the German Army even over the roughest terrain.

was one of the few vehicles which could cope with the extreme conditions of heat, cold and mud found in the Russian campaign.

The winner of this particular race was the American army. As early as 1925 it had used a commercial chassis and platform with four bucket seats fixed to it. The grandfather of the Jeep was a four-wheel drive vehicle, designed by Arthur Herrington of the Marmon–Harrington company, later famous for its truck (see page 127). Ford took up his idea for a 4x4 half-ton truck, although in the end it was smaller than the first design.

The father of the Jeep was none other than the ubiquitous Austin 7. Before the war it had been built in Japan and by BMW in Germany and was brought to the United States by the small firm of Bantam. The other parent was a remarkable military engineer, Col Robert G. Howie. In 1937 he took an Austin 7 engine supplied by Bantam and installed it in a vehicle so close to the ground that it became known as the 'bellyflopper'.

Bantam's loan of three adapted Austin 7s to the National Guard to show off their potential for military reconnaissance led the army to define its requirements more closely. In June 1940, a sub-

committee including Howie started to lay down the criteria for a vehicle which would have four-wheel drive, a crew of three, could be armed with a 7.62mm (30in) machine-gun, a minimum speed of 3mph (5kph) and ground clearance of 16cm (6 in) – the lesson of the bellyflopper had clearly sunk in.

When the proposal was put out for tender the rules were stringent. The maximum weight was to be a mere 1,300lb (590kg) and the payload 600lb (272kg). To make matters worse the contestants were expected to deliver seventy vehicles in a mere seventy-five days, including eight with four-wheel steering, a requirement which was soon dropped.

Only two companies even entered the race, Bantam and Willys. Bantam hired a brilliant engineer, Karl K. Probst, who drew up the plans for what was to emerge as the Jeep in a mere five days. He then put together a prototype using a 48bhp Continental engine and Spicer transmission. The only problem was the weight, which was 550lb (250kg) above the army's ridiculously low limit.

Willys couldn't make the time limit (they were afraid they couldn't get the parts in time from Spicer). Their initial quoted price was lower but rose above the Bantam estimate when the penalty for late submission was taken into account. So Bantam got the contract and submitted the prototype before the end of September, a mind-bogglingly short time. But by then, the army's natural predilection for established suppliers entered the equation and engineers from both Willys and Ford were allowed to watch the Bantam being tested. Nevertheless, the first order, for 1,500 vehicles went to Bantam despite the protests of the Quartermaster's Corps.

When the QMC was allowed to place orders for the same number of vehicles from Ford and Willys, both responded with ones that were naturally very similar to the Bantam prototype. The Willys Quad had a superior engine but was far

too heavy. Their engineers made a brave decision, to reduce weight on the rest of the machine (the changes even included the paint) to ensure that they kept their engine, nicknamed the 'Go Devil.'

In the end, Willys were able to meet the tight final specifications, which included a maximum speed of 55mph (88.5kph), the ability to ford rivers 18ins (46cm) deep, and a maximum weight of 2,100lb (853kg) while carrying 800lb (363kg). And that is the shape in which the Jeep went into production, albeit with a few minor changes like adding an axe and a spade and increasing the capacity of the fuel tank from ten to fifteen US gallons (56.8 litres). Willys made 361,349 Jeeps before the end of the war and Ford, the loser, nearly a quarter of a million. And Bantam, the inventor of the whole idea? They were left out in the cold on the excuse that they didn't have the necessary manufacturing capacity.

After the war Willys were prevented from advertising that they alone had invented the Jeep, but retained the by now legendary brand name while poor Bantam went broke in 1956. After many vicissitudes, the name is now the property of Chrysler Motors, which uses it for a variety of vehicles far more luxurious than the spartan original.

And the name? The starters included Bug, Midget, Peep, Blitz Buggy and Quad. The final name was probably first used by Willys' test driver to distinguish between his firm's prototype and that made by Ford.

And why 'Jeep'? The most convincing of the many explanations proffered since then is that the test driver was thinking of a strange animal called Eugene the Jeep, introduced into the Popeye strip cartoon in 1936. The animal was almost as big as a dog, came from Africa, ate nothing but orchids and was able to make itself invisible. It soon became popular and as a result anything astonishing soon came to be described as a Jeep.

Chapter Six

TO THE RESCUE

As SOCIETIES CHANGE, so do the emergencies with which they are faced, and the means of response. There's an enormous gulf between the hand- or horse-drawn carts scurrying to the scenes of fires in Victorian London and the ultra-sophisticated equipment performing the same task today when an oil refinery or skyscraper catches fire. Firefighters have to be equipped with pumps and ladders of ever-increasing length, together with breathing equipment and chemical foams. In firefighting, as in so many other fields, the twentieth century has been one of growing specialization in equipment, training and outlook.

There's an equally cavernous gulf between the handcarts used in former times to rush patients to hospital and today's ambulances, fitted with advanced equipment and manned by paramedics who probably know more medicine than did qualified doctors 100 years ago.

Although all this equipment, and the techniques, are outside the scope of this book, the evolution of the vehicles used to get it all to the scene are both intriguing and relevant. The emergency services were a natural target for makers of even the earliest motorized vehicles. Speed of response far outweighed the cost of running the vehicles.

Steam was first used in firefighting, not to power the fire engines, but the pumps. In 1873, for instance, a new Firemaster in Edinburgh not only introduced new uniforms but also the first steam-powered pump, drawn inevitably by horses. 'The spectacle of these machines racing to an alarm call was awe-inspiring,' wrote Bart Vanderveen.[1]

> With furnace aglow, smoke belching forth and crew clinging like limpets, the appliance would thunder along the streets to the accompaniment of the traditional call, 'Hi ya hi' from the crewmen, a legacy, it is said, of the days when firemen were all former seamen. The use of bugles, posthorns and even police whistles was not uncommon, but by 1905 the gong or bell had become more or less universal.

In 1892, as part of his attempts to find uses for his engines, Gottfried Daimler introduced a motorized pump for use in horse-drawn fire engines. The pump was less than half the weight of a comparable steam-driven model, it didn't require the time to get up steam and it could be operated by two men, whereas hand pumps demanded a crew of thirty-two. In 1895 it was seen in England demonstrating its capacity to pump water at a rate of 300 gallons (1,364 litres) a minute to a height of 98ft (30m). In the United States, the very earliest trucks were built as fire apparatus, including the vehicles designed to haul a pump or tall ladder to the scene of the fire. Some made

(Opposite) Steam-powered pumps were invaluable even in horse-drawn fire engines.

The Keystone Cops testing
the traction of the Model T
Ford to its limit.

in the 1880s had internal combustion engines, although many ran on rails or tracks and had no steering of their own.

Steam was never a contender in the race. The first self-propelled steam apparatus was built by Paul R. Hodge in 1902. Unfortunately, steam pumps or engines had to be kept permanently on steam (although some boiler heaters were marketed for fire stations). However, a few steam-powered appliances were delivered to British brigades as late as the first world war and one or two even survived to help fight the Blitz, and Merryweather, one of the major producers of steam appliances, subsequently became a famous name in motorized fire engines. (In 1908 it became the first manufacturer to use power from the engine for the ladder.)

In Britain the first motorized appliances were commissioned by the Liverpool and Eccles brigades, while the first petrol-driven motor pump, made by Merryweather, was delivered to the French Rothschilds to protect their enormous *château* at Ferrières.

Inevitably the period before the first world war was one of improvisation, with manufacturers tacking the rear of a steam pumper on to a petrol-engined machine. In 1908, for instance, A.C. Webb, a motor-racing ace, converted a Thames Flyer touring-car chassis into a motor pump. The Americans even developed a sophisticated system of 'flying squadrons' mounted on touring-car chassis and carrying a few hand extinguishers in advance of the (inevitably slower) fire brigade itself.

The interwar period was the one in which appliances and services took shape in their modern form. Ambulances were developed for civilians, but, typically, the service was rationed: it cost 'the magic half a crown' – the equivalent of 12½p (19c), worth over £5 ($8) today – for a patient to use the service. The ambulances were still primitive, to say the least, many were merely glorified versions of the 'fever wagons' previously used to take patients to hospital. Terry Spurr, a veteran of the London Ambulance and Emergency Service, recalls that the older ones were veritable death traps: 'You were more likely to die after travelling in one of them than before – horrendous cross-infections.'

But even newly developed vehicles were not entirely satisfactory. Another former London ambulanceman, Charles Gallehawk, remembers how the early Vauxhall ambulances had a nasty habit of overturning on corners, while early Austins were so high that it was terribly difficult to load stretchers on to them. Both Austin and Morris soon adapted their mass-produced commercial vehicles to the requirements of the service.

One major problem in the early days was ambulance drivers who couldn't cope with crash gearboxes, hence the early introduction of automatic transmission, especially in London, where the shorter runs meant constant gear-changing and made the increased fuel consumption resulting from automatic boxes or the preselector boxes made as early as the 1930s by Talbot rather irrelevant.

All and any technical advances were welcome. Better suspensions meant a more comfortable ride for patients, while fire brigades eagerly welcomed diesel engines when they were introduced in 1934 because they started more easily in cold weather. Not that the firefighters themselves were comfortable: they were still perched on unprotected seats on top or outside of the machine, an inheritance from the days of steam* hanging on grimly as their unwieldy machines squalled round corners on their solid rubber tyres. As one fireman from those days recalls: 'We felt like Roman gladiators out there, hanging on with our brass helmets shining above us.' It was only in 1931 that municipal brigades started to receive enclosed machines.

In the first world war every type of vehicle was pressed into service for carrying the wounded: two Model Ts each side of a Renault.

Much of the equipment, in Britain anyway, was still impro-vised. Trailer fire pumps were used in rural areas because they could be got to lakes, ponds and streams inaccessible to ortho-dox appliances, while motorcycle combinations were trans-formed into miniature three-wheeled fire 'enginettes' (do not mock, they could carry 1,000ft (305m) of hose, short extension ladders or chemical extinguishers).

However, a handful of manufacturers were emerging as spe-cialist producers. In Germany Magirus, the truck makers had produced the first turntable ladder, a 90ft (27.5m) model, as early as 1892, and continued to specialize in pumps and engines. These would usually have been equipped with the 100ft (30.5m) wooden ladders made by the German specialists, Metz, and pumps capable of delivering 900 gallons (4,091 litres) of water a minute.

In Britain, Merryweather and Dennis were the great names. Dennis, still an independent concern today, has a long history. John Downing came from Fowler's in 1902, having served an apprenticeship with steam. He had driven Dennis cars in trials and, according to the firm's historian, Stuart Brown, was 'never more at home than when he was putting new ideas to paper in the drawing office'. The company went public in 1913 and soon abandoned cars. During the first world war it built 7,000 trucks for the war office and since then has specialized in fire engines, muni-cipal vehicles and, more recently, a nice line in small sin-gle-decker 'midi-buses', somewhat larger than minibuses.

Downing, like all innovators, enjoyed showing off the power of his machines. He took two engines with turbine pumps to St Paul's to show the London County Council, which controlled the country's biggest brigade, the capabilities of the Dennis machines. Coupled together they threw a jet of water right over the dome (in 1911, Puch, the Austro–Daimler subsidiary, sup-plied the corporation of Vienna with a water sprinkler which doubled up as a fire engine, boasting that it could send a jet over the town hall). In the United States, Ahrens–Fox made a Rolls–Royce of a machine with a huge pump mounted ahead of the engine.

In Britain the chaotic nature of local government was reflected in the haphazard arrangements for coping with disas-ters. In many places a single service provided both ambulances and firefighting services. It was the Blitz in London and then bombing throughout the country that transformed public atti-tudes and the management, control and equipment of both services. It had to, for at the outbreak of war there were no fewer than 1,600 separate fire brigades in England and Wales offering a very varied level of service. These utilities had to be reinforced by the creation of the Auxiliary Fire Service. Despite early sniping – notably centred on the view that mem-bers of the AFS were avoiding their patriotic duty – the scale of the Blitz brought home the realization that the AFS was playing a crucial role.

This 1905 Wolseley ambulance was at least faster and less uncomfortable than its horse-drawn predecessors.

The standard Bedford ambulance in a rehearsal for the Blitz.

The same spirit of improvisation prevailed as far as equipment was concerned. Pumps and water tenders were hauled by any vehicle with the necessary power and which could be fitted with a towing bar: hearses, delivery vans, small lorries, even large cars. A borough engineer's lorry could serve as a fire engine with the attachment of a trailer pump. Other vehicles were often simply fitted with spring loaded overrun brakes and rear illumination (sometimes provided by oil lamps). In the most spectacular instance, over 2,000 London taxis were requisitioned as ATCs (auxiliary towing cars), complete with drivers, who could find their way to the most obscure troublespots.

Later on some specialized vehicles were developed, notably two-ton Austins and one-ton (1,016kg) Fords. New ladders were based on bus chassis made by Dennis or Leyland. An increasing number of mobile war tenders were able to carry water to fires well away from hydrants or rivers (one of the worst nights of the Blitz was when the Germans bombed at a low tide).

The war, and the setting up of the National Health Service, resulted in a proper structure for both services and the firefighters were obliged to work within the standards set by the Home Office (which included one Blitz-derived requirement that appliances should carry at least 400 gallons (1,818 litres) of water. Standardization did not prevent some disasters, notably attempts to build perfect ambulances. With bodywork made by specialists like Hooper or Barker, they proved impractical, over-engineered, far too expensive, or all three. Terry Spurr emphasizes the luxury: single doors that clunked shut, brass handles and steps which automatically folded out when the door was opened. In the end the market was largely cornered by specially adapted

commercial vehicles, like those made by Bedford (in France the same role is performed by specially adapted large Citroën cars, ideal ambulances because of their soft air suspension).

Fire brigades needed more specialized equipment and it was Daimler–Benz which produced the first truly modern appliance. As early as 1949 it introduced the MB-Metz LF25, with a demountable hose reel, fire hooks, ladders and smoke-extraction equipment. In Britain the county-wide fire brigades concentrated on two marques, Leyland and Dennis. In the 1950s Dennis introduced two models, the F8 with a smaller pump, and the F12 with a wheeled escape, which enthusiasts describe as 'the last real fire engines', although that accolade should surely go to the F24, introduced in 1961, which cost £4,500 ($6,750). Such a machine, with its eight-cylinder Rolls-Royce engine and automatic gearbox, could reach 70mph (113kph), and last a full fifteen years (with four more as a reserve vehicle).

But oddest of all, and most famous, were the Green Goddesses. These were basically Bedford S Types with a 35ft (11m) extending ladder capable of pumping 1,000 gallons (4,546 litres) a minute. They were originally designed to be used in the event of fires caused by atom bombs, and were trundled out for (rather ineffectual) use when Britain's firefighters went on strike in 1981.

* A seating arrangement named the Braidwood, after James Braidwood, a famous head of the London Fire Brigade.

(Opposite, top) The Daimler, the ultimate in (expensive, clumsy, over-engineered) London ambulances of the postwar era.

(Opposite, below) In 1937 this Dennis apparatus was the very latest piece of equipment for rescuing the wealthy inhabitants of Belgrave Square.

(Left) Grimmest of tasks: a Black Maria taking John Christie from the back door of the court where he was charged with the murder of his wife (and five other women) in 1952.

Chapter Seven

THE VERY DIFFERENT UNITED STATES

THE UNITED STATES is different, very different. A trucker can start his journey in the sub-tropical climate of Texas, filling up with summerweight fuel and lubricating oil and thus become completely bogged down in the wintry conditions prevailing at the same time in the Dakotas. The result has been extraordinary trucks developed to tackle the country's immense distances and contrasting conditions and the design parameters imposed by legislation. Physically, they are indeed the glamorous monsters seen in so many films, TV series and advertisements, with almost all their visible parts – bonnets, cabs, exhausts, fuel tanks and bumpers – made of gleaming aluminium.

Industrially the scene is also distinctive: virtually all American truck makers, unlike most of their European or Japanese counterparts, are basically assemblers. As a result operators large and small can ensure that their trucks remain personalized to an extent now unknown outside the USA. This helps the smaller manufacturers to compete much more easily than their European equivalents. This personalization, however, applies only to the top end of the truck business, the so-called Class 8 vehicles of over 30,000lbs (13,608kg). (Today they usually weigh 80,000lbs [36,288kg]). In Classes 1 to 7, covering lighter trucks, Ford and General Motors enjoy the same advantages of scale and vertical integration as the major European firms. Chrysler and the Japanese manufacturers, Honda Toyota and Nissan, have made major inroads into the market for that all-American speciality the pick-up truck. But in Class 8 individualism rules, OK.

So does Darwin, for the survivors are the remnants of an enormous field which at the start of the century went right through the alphabet from Acme, Aetna, Alco and All American to Wilcox, Winther, Wolverine and Yellow–Knight. But today three firms (Ford, the GM subsidiary GMC and International Harvester) dominate the general truck market, while three others, Paccar (owners of Kenworth and Peterbilt), Mack and Freightliner dispute the top end. Ford is the only one of the big three to retain an important presence in the sector where, unusually, the Japanese have made virtually no impact.

Yet, the story can also be seen as a triumph for the continental European way of doing business. The problems of the late 1970s allowed Renault, Volvo and Mercedes–Benz to acquire three famous names, Mack, White and Freightliner, and thus to gain a solid position in an industry where they had previously had little impact with imported trucks, precisely because conditions and requirements were so different from those of most of their other major markets.

The glamour of modern American aluminium trucks.

A continuing tradition of individualism ensures that buyers' options are not confined to engines and gearboxes. They include batteries, starters, fuel tanks and drivers' seating, and drivers add their own personal touches with graffiti and 'rolling paintings'. Manufacturers take the drivers seriously. In the 1950s the then small firm of Freightliner based its advertising on the idea of being 'ODM engineered' – for the benefit of owners, drivers and mechanics, to whom the firm did indeed listen attentively. Nevertheless, the biggest seller today is the Transtar, made by International Harvester, a truck without any of the glamour which attracts independent operators but one which is preferred by fleet owners because it is cheaper to operate.

In the beginning, all the manufacturers made both trucks and cars as a matter of course. Early truck makers included such names as Pierce–Arrow and Oldsmobile, whose founder, Ransom E. Olds, went on to found a famous truck maker, Reo, while Henry Ford started his working life as chief engineer for the Detroit brand of truck made for a few years around the turn of the century.

The new vehicles were heavily promoted with events like the 1,700-mile (2,736-km) Munsey Tour of 1910 (one successful contestant was called the Strenuous Randolph after its makers, who went under three years later). Even then the advertising was splendid: 'Why feed your profits to your horses?' was one slogan.

Many general engineering companies like Marmon (see page 127) started to build vehicles but the most powerful outsider was the McCormick Harvesting Machine Company, the world leader in reapers. In 1902 it combined with a number of its major competitors to form the International Harvester Company. The firm got out of the motor-car business before the first world war but is still one of the leaders in the truck market.

International first produced the high-wheeled Auto Buggy, cleverly designed to look as much like a horse-drawn buggy as possible. It was aimed at helping McCormick's customers to haul produce to the nearest market or railhead (and the family to church on Sunday) over the truly terrible tracks universal in rural America at the time. Then came the Autowagons, made

International Harvester tempted its customers away from their horse-drawn transport by naming its first petrol-driven vehicle a Buggy.

Around 1910, Saurer trucks were imported from Switzerland, and then assembled in the same New Jersey factory which made Mack Bulldogs.

on what was described as a 'radical' progressive assembly line, and in 1915 IH introduced low-wheeled F trucks, which looked like modern trucks. In 1923 the company opened what was destined to become the world's largest truck plant in Fort Wayne, Indiana, using mass-production methods and an assembly line for the first time to produce six-wheel vehicles, first the Model 52, then the first trucks to offer pneumatic tyres. In 1929 IH installed an early and sophisticated proving ground.

IH was following the industry's general pattern. The vast increase in vehicle production during the first world war inevitably led to a postwar slump, but sales rebounded from 97,000 in 1920 to four times that level a mere three years later. They reached a peak of 609,000 in 1926 but had started to decline even before the onset of the slump. The trucks themselves were steadily improved. To take one simple example: by 1922 more trucks were produced with metal wheels than with wooden ones and by 1926 sales of pneumatic tyres had overtaken those of the solid types. Five years later some states had started to ban any other kind.

Uses became more specialized: the decade saw the development of the tractor-trailer combination, originally designed for loggers. By 1922 there were even 'rolling grocery stores'. Today there are rolling stores for every need – haircutting, pet care, domestic cleaners, rolling laundromats, rolling churches, and a

truck which can offer a selection of prepared foods ranging from a sandwich to a three-course meal.

Following the election of Franklin Delano Roosevelt as President in late 1932 and the launching of the New Deal, projects organized by the WPA (Works Progress Administration) and the great growth of the federal highway programme helped ensure that road transport and thus truck-building recovered from the Depression sooner than many other industrial sectors. Indeed, production was up to nearly 900,000 by 1937, 50 per cent above the top level of the 1920s.

But with growth came regulation by the federal government. In 1932 the Federal Motor Carrier Act gave the Interstate Commerce Commission (which already regulated the railways) power over interstate trucks. The American Trucking Association soon fought back, arguing for self-regulation. But the next year the ICC created a division, backed by twenty district offices, to regulate the industry. In 1937 came new safety regulations.

These seemed revolutionary at the time, though incredibly elementary today – for instance, trucks had to have two headlamps, tail lamps and a stop lamp.

Individual states complicated matters by introducing their own regulations. These ranged from an (unenforceable) limitation on drivers' hours to a wide variety of limits on the size, length and weight of trucks. This had considerable influence on the manufacturers. After the first world war, for instance, Freightliner deliberately designed its WF-42 model so that it could pull two 24ft (7.3m) trailers and yet comply with the 60ft (18.3m) overall length limit then in effect in most western states. A later model featured a Cummins engine mounted horizontally under the frame and behind the cab so that operators could use a 24ft (7.3m) freight box rather than a 22ft (6.7m) one in the appropriate states.

During the 1930s the trucks themselves changed, especially in appearance. For the first time trucks began to lose their purely utilitarian look as streamlining came into vogue. IH was in the forefront in technical terms. They added a second rear axle in 1935, grabbing long-term leadership in the twenty-ton field, and used new strengthened pneumatic tyres.

The decade also saw the first stages of a major shift in truck manufacture. Originally, the specialist vehicle makers had been concentrated in states such as New York – described as a 'hot-bed of early truck development activities'[1] – and Wisconsin, where there were nearly 100 manufacturers when Oshkosh, the only survivor, started in business.

By contrast three of today's majors, Kenworth, Paccar and Freightliner, are based in the west, a success story that is based on the requirements of major customers on the west coast. Typically, Kenworth, founded in 1915 in Portland, Oregon as

the Gerlinger Motor Car Company, started life as a pure assembler, even contracting out the manufacture of the cabs. The Kenworth legend derived from the truck it made from 1916 until 1923. It was called the 'Gersix' because its engine had six cylinders and it could carry 6,000lb (2,722kg). It sold for $4,000 (£2,667), double the price of a Mack.

The firm went broke in 1917 and was rescued in 1923 by Messrs Kent and Worthington, who combined their names in the relaunched venture. From the start it obeyed the rules which seem to have been followed by successful truck manufacturers: it would build trucks to the specific requirements of even the smallest customer (by 1926 it was offering six different models, a number that doubled by the end of the decade), all designed for hauliers on the Pacific coast, where the distances

The Mack AB, predecessor of the beloved AC, used to serve the American restlessness.

IC REFRIGERATOR

RIS

COMPANY

TIONAL REFRIGERATOR
· CAR COMPANY ·

BAXTER BARSMITH SYSTEM
BUILDERS CHICAGO ILL.

By 1918, a cab-over-engined truck could be used with a surprisingly long trailer.

The 1926 Model T in one of its innumerable guises, as a mobile fruit stall.

were far too great, and the conditions far too rugged, for trucks designed for the easier conditions encountered on the east coast. By then its products included buses, fire engines and delivery trucks.

So it was natural for Kenworth to become the first American manufacturer to instal diesel engines as original equipment, which it did in 1932. These were chosen (and not just by Kenworth – IH was another early diesel enthusiast with the D-300 variant of its D series) not so much because they were economical (fuel prices were still incredibly low) as for their superior torque and thus greatly increased pulling power on gradients. In 1941

Kenworth installed the world's first all-aluminium diesel engine, a challenge to which Freightliner responded in 1949 by fitting a 275hp Cummins supercharged diesel engine to its 'Bubblenose' model. By 1944 Kenworth had developed a chassis frame made of extruded aluminium as well as using the metal in cabs, bonnets and transmission casings. The company was also a pioneer of such innovations as six-wheel drive, air brakes and rear-axle torsion-bar suspension.

Kenworth's story is paralleled by that of the Peterbilt. In 1939 a lumberman, Al Peterman, bought the Fageol Motor Car Company, which had been building luxury cars in Oakland,

California since 1915. The next year he produced a heavy-duty truck, which he christened The Peterbilt, for use in his own industry. In 1944 the business was sold to a group of employees. Today Peterbilt remains the (expensive) favourite of drivers.

Even the biggest firms had to go out of their way to cater to individual tastes. Typically, IH offered sixty-six versions of its L series in 1949, while the R series introduced three years later included 168 chassis models and a variety of wheelbase lengths for weights of between half a ton and twenty tons, called Loadstar and Roadstar. The 'Star' name stuck and a new range, Navistar, introduced in 1982, is now better known than IH itself.

Both Kenworth and Peterbilt are now subsidiaries of Paccar, another company from the same tradition of supplying rugged equipment for use by lumbermen. Founded in 1905 as Seattle Car Manufacturing to produce railway and logging equipment, by 1909 it had made the first railroad cars able to carry the longest and heaviest logs. A 1917 merger led to a change of name to the Pacific Car and Foundry Company, hence Paccar. In the 1930s the founder's son bought back the firm and bought up Carco, a major producer of power winches. Paccar bought Kenworth in 1945 and Dart and Peterbilt in 1958.

In recent years their fastest-growing rival has been Freightliner, which fits the same pattern. It was actually founded by a major operator, Leland James, the owner of Consolidated Freight Lines. Since he had founded the company in 1929 he had customized many parts and rebuilt trucks to find ways of cutting costs and weight, notably by using aluminium. In 1939 James set up a new manufacturing company, supported by some key suppliers. Because of the 'assembly'

The local Coca-Cola bottler in New Orleans could shift a lot of bottles in this late-model Mack Bulldog of 1926.

tradition in heavy American trucks, manufacturers of key parts like engines (Cummins) or axles and transmissions (Rockwell, Eaton and, later, Fuller) play a crucial, if largely unsung role in American industry.

Even though Freightliner was producing only a handful of trucks after the war, James's power was such that he appeared to be a potential threat to other manufacturers, who prevented key component suppliers from supplying him directly. He responded with elaborate deals through distributors to obtain axles, engines and transmissions.

Mack, the most famous of the traditional manufacturers, was different from its rivals mainly in that it was the only specialist which made most of its own major components like engines and gearboxes. The firm still met the same regulation and customer

requirements: the postwar H model was particularly successful as a tractor because of its short length when measured from the front bumper to the back of the cab. It was therefore able to use high-volume square-nosed trailers within length limits. Mack also claims more innovations than any other single producer, including power steering, power brakes, the use of rubber for engine and transmission mounts, air cleaners, filters, the constant horsepower diesel engine, offset cabs and directed water flow for improved cooling. Moreover, Mack claims that its in-house transmissions, which provide between five and eighteen speeds, are better able to stand up to heavy haulage than those of its rivals.

All the major specialists naturally vied to be the first to introduce new design features, including the lighter trucks required to

Even as late as 1959, International was not offering diesel power – although its range could be powered by LPG (Liquid Petroleum Gas).

This White 300 delivery truck, photographed in Philadelphia in 1970, was working for Horn & Hardart, then a household name in food and snackbars.

meet weight limits. All of them claim they were the first to use aluminum on a large scale, especially in cabs, and were among the first to offer cab-over-engine designs to counteract length limits. Later they competed to produce cabs which tilted to allow easier access to the engine. At the end of the 1950s, Freightliner and Peterbilt introduced hoods which tilted the full ninety degrees – Freightliner's design incorporated their own patented pump to complete the ninety-degree tilt in a mere thirty-eight seconds.

Like other major manufacturers worldwide, they also experimented with the gas turbine, a favourite novelty of the 1950s and 1960s. Kenworth, for example, installed a gas-turbine engine made by Boeing in an experimental truck as early as 1950. These engines were lighter – Freightliner, also using a Boeing engine, found that the experimental TurboLiner they built in 1965 weighed 2,400lbs (1,089kg) less than a comparable diesel-engined vehicle – but both manufacturers found that gas turbines were too unreliable and too thirsty to be a practical proposition even before the hike in fuel prices following the first oil crisis in 1973–74 put paid to the whole idea.

The trend in making trucks for long-distance haulage benefited from a boom set off by the Interstate and Defense Highway Act of 1956, which authorized the construction of over 42,000 miles of highway linking virtually every major city in the country. The resulting upsurge lasted (with a hiccup during the 1973–74 oil crisis) until 1979, and its length and apparent permanence lulled too many manufacturers into a dangerous state of complacency.

Yet even during the good years Darwinisim was at work. In 1950 there were still forty truck manufacturers in the US. A few years later the number was down to ten, but then even the most famous names tended to be relatively small. In 1958 White bought the legendary Diamond T firm for a mere $10 million, not surprisingly, given that after the merger it was still producing only 2,500 trucks a year. In 1968 White also bought the earth-moving firm of Euclid, this time from General Motors, which, since the war, had been steadily withdrawing from making heavy or unusual vehicles. By contrast Ford made a splashy entry into the market for heavy-duty trucks in 1960 by offering the first 100,000-mile (160,930-km) warranty. Ford's impact grew after the introduction in 1980 of its 'Longnose' model which featured an original suspension system.

All over the world long-distance lorry drivers are the heirs to a long and romantic tradition going back to the carters and drovers of prerailway days. But, inevitably, given the scale of the continent, the home of the cult is the United States, whose icons range from *Cannonball*, the popular TV series which uses trucks made by GM to the close-knit community of truckers with their own citizens' band radio network.

The drivers even had their own cafés, the famous 'truck stops'. These began to appear in the 1930s and 1940s when the fleets switched to diesel fuel, which was unavailable at normal gas stations. They developed because of the truckers' attitude. In the words of Roger King of the National Association of Truck Stops: 'The truckers see themselves as skilled and professional and look down on cars whose drivers don't want to mix with truckers anyway.'

Less romantic were the Teamsters: originally they were drivers of local drayage wagons pulled by 'teams' of horses. But by the 1950s they had developed into a branch of the Mafia, the subject of endless congressional investigations and prosecutions by the FBI, culminating in the violent death of their fabled leader, Jimmy Hoffa.

The world of truckers and their trucks received a series of jolts at the end of the 1970s which transformed the scene. The first signs of impending emergency came with the 1973–74 oil crisis. The problems were compounded by record interest rates, soaring inflation and, above all, legislation: the government decreed that a new costly and controversial antiskid braking system had to be fitted to all models made in 1975, a regulation which induced buyers to bring forward their orders. By the time the manufacturers had started to instal the system the market had collapsed (Freightliner's sales dropped by two-thirds). Even though the requirement was eventually overturned in the courts the warning shots had been fired.

The latter part of the 1970s was full of reorganizations and new deals: for instance, Freightliner ended its distribution agreement with White and signed up to sell Volvo's larger

Eat your heart out Pirelli – the Americans got there first in this publicity shot for Kenworth.

How Kenworth envisaged
the classic Truckstop.

Refrigerated trucks were crucial for firms like the 'Chicago Fish House'.

trucks. But this was as nothing compared with the upheavals induced by the 1980 crisis. This was a rerun of 1973–74 except that the recession was even deeper, exacerbated by soaring interest rates and the industry's deregulation through the Motor Carrier Act. The focus for the changes was the abolition of the need to obtain the expensive and difficult 'authority' to haul certain commodities on most long-distance interstate routes. Naturally, the independents were all for deregulation, while the carriers, the trucking companies, and the Teamsters were against it because it would upset their cosy set-up.

Enter a new and only sketchily organized union, headed by Mark Parkhurst, the editor of *Overdrive* magazine. A wildcat protest ensued, taking 75,000 trucks (three quarters of the total operated by independents) off the road. As a result President Carter started the process which led to the lifting of the 'iron curtain' on weight – the restrictions on heavy hauliers. The result greatly reduced the power of the Teamsters, already

weakened by twenty years of government harassment and a widening gulf between the carriers and the independents, whose sense of solidarity was reinforced by the lead-up to deregulation.

Faced with such upheavals, White Motors filed for bankruptcy while International Harvester faced massive financial problems. But the crisis provided the more financally solid Europeans with the chance to dominate the industry. White's bankruptcy led to a takeover by Volvo, which went on to buy GM's heavy truck division in 1988. In 1983 Renault increased its stake in Mack from 20 to 50 percent while Freightliner's parent company sold the concern to Daimler–Benz for $260 million (£173.3 million).

Freightliner had struggled through the postwar boom but had found its feet with the FLC 1200 series of trucks introduced in 1979, which proved highly fuel efficient in the second oil crisis. Daimler was already a major presence in the US market for smaller vehicles but required a local partner to succeed with the big ones. The partnership has enabled Freightliner to become the single biggest brand in heavy trucks, helped by new models introduced in 1988 which relied on the parent company's wind tunnel for the design of aerodynamic components like the front bumper. That year Freightliner accounted for a third of the heavy trucks sold by Daimler–Benz worldwide and has emerged as a jumping-off point for executives destined for top engineering jobs elsewhere in the group.

Of the native specialist manufacturers, only Paccar thrived, and by 1989 its two marques combined made it the largest manufacturer of heavy trucks in the country. It also expanded outside the United States. In 1966 it had already set up in Australia, in the early 1980s it bought the venerable British firm of Foden and expanded into Malaysia a few years later.

The Europeans had timed their purchases perfectly. In 1983 a new piece of legislation, the Transportation Assistance Act, had accelerated the pace of deregulation and allowed operators to use twin-trailer combinations and vehicles with a gross weight of up to 80,000lbs (36,288kg) on interstate highways. It also ended decades of anarchy by forbidding individual states to set their own individual limits on the lengths of tractor– trailer combinations, a relaxation which caused a shift back from cab-over-engine designs to conventional bonneted vehicles.

Deregulation also made a profound impact on the trucking industry. The strain of competition has affected the operators and the drivers as much as the manufacturers. Of the top 100 carriers in 1980, only eighteen remained in business fourteen years later. Moreover, standards have slipped – one in seven of all trucks inspected by state patrols were found to have defective brakes. In the early 1980s the average trucker drove for forty hours a week. The average is now twice that: time has become much more important and schedules are crucial. People break the rules as a matter of course because the legislation, which dates back to the 1930s, is hopelessly out of date.

To make matters worse the distances are mind-boggling: the average haulage length is over 2,000 miles (3,219km) – from London to Istanbul and back. Typically, a team in a sleeper truck drives from coast to coast in a mere three days, each driver taking a six-hour shift, stopping only for food and fuel. One in ten long-haul drivers regularly use drugs like Dexedrine and Methadrine. Not surprisingly, driver fatigue is a major factor in accidents involving commercial vehicles.

Even when the trucks stop there are problems with waiting to load and unload. Today 'lumpers' – groups of itinerant labourers – make themselves available to meet the trucks. But there has also been a rise in 'coercive lumping', when gangs put such pressure on the drivers that sometimes they have to load and unload themselves.

It is not surprising, then, that some carriers are experiencing a shortage of drivers and a turnover in driving staff of 100 percent a year. The entry fee for independents is high since bankers are unwilling to lend money to a first-time truck purchaser. So some carriers offer a form of 'lease purchase' which forces the driver–leasers to earn the necessary instalments through ferociously long hours. Critics claim that this is merely a modern form of indentured servitude which enables trucking firms to exploit dreamers and greenhorns.

Now, irony of ironies, the industry has turned to its historic rivals, the railroads, for help. Some of the major carriers, notably Schneider and J.B. Hunt, are using them for the bulk of the haul, relying on their own trucks only for the regional distribution. This new-found alliance between former bitter enemies, like everything else about the industry, remains typically American, allowing the very best – the possibility of self-advancement, of small-scale entrepreneurialism – as well as every type of ruthless capitalist exploitation to flourish.

A Mack Bulldog in New York City, the original home of the firm, in 1917, after it had moved out to its present home in Allenstown, Pennsylvania.

THE RELATIONSHIP BETWEEN American drivers and their trucks is so personal that many of the best known have acquired nicknames. The big trucks originally made by IH at its plant in Emeryville California continued to be called 'Emeryvilles' long after production had shifted elsewhere. One of Freightliner's early trucks was called the Shovelnose and a later model the Bubblenose. But the most famous nickname of them all was the Bulldog, made by Mack for twenty-four years, the longest production run of any American truck.

Mack had been established by five brothers who were second-generation German-Americans. In the early 1900s Jack, in particular, foresaw the growth in mechanical transport and started to convert their blacksmith's shop in Brooklyn to suit the production of trucks. Their first covered a million miles. In 1904 they made a twenty-four-seat charabanc which they called the Manhattan. In 1906 Mack produced the first truck with the driver's seat over the engine, the forerunner of the cab-over-engine design, and a year later a seven-ton dump truck used extensively in building the New York subway system. Another pioneering effort was a two-ton 'junior' model introduced in 1913 which presaged modern delivery vehicles.

In 1905 Mack moved to Allenstown in Pennsylvania and introduced the AC. It had a four-cylinder, 75hp, gravity-fed petrol engine with high-tension magneto ignition and a pressed-steel chassis frame. It was driven through a three-speed selective-sliding transmission via a jackshaft through double side chains to solid tyres. But its most distinctive feature was the unusual bonnet and radiator between the engine and the driver, who had the benefit of an all-steel cab with an optional metal roof – a revolution at a time when most trucks merely had wooden box seats unprotected from the elements.

Large numbers of the AC were sent to the British forces in France, who promptly renamed it the Bulldog for its durability and tenacity. The name was absorbed to the extent that the Bulldog symbol has become part of the vernacular. Indeed, in prefeminist days 'built like a Mack truck' was used of any square-shaped lady.

SMALL AND BEAUTIFUL

MARMON, THE SMALLEST and most recherché truck maker in the USA, started life as a manufacturer of corn-milling equipment. The firm made its first car in 1904 and won the first Indianapolis 500 in 1911 at an amazing average speed of 80mph (129kph). Marmon stopped building its luxury cars during the Depression. Later, in the 1930s, Arthur Harrington, who made trucks under the name Marmon–Harrington, was responsible for the 'grandfather of the Jeep' (see page 101).

During and after the second world war, Marmon concentrated on specialist vehicles: half-tracks, plane refuelling trucks and the like. In 1963 the company moved to Texas and started to produce tailormade trucks, making full use of aluminium and, above all, fibreglass in the cabs. This policy has continued since 1974 ,when Marmon was bought by an entrepreneur, Stratton Georgoulis, a chemical engineer who trained at the Massachusetts Institute of Technology.

Every one of the 700 Marmons sold (or rather presold) every year is different. Marmon offers a standard power train – a Caterpillar or Cummins diesel coupled to a twin-plate clutch, thirteen-speed Fuller transmission and a Rockwell bogie. But otherwise the choice is huge including four different styles of hood and five cabs. If owners want some small changes (one wanted the baggage compartment under the cab moved) – well, the customer is king, although Marmon is careful to keep its prices close to those of that other 'king of

The Marmon, tailor-made in Texas and used in tough conditions world-wide. This one is hauling sugar cane to the mill in Cali, Colombia.

the road', Peterbilt. 'People are sick of dealing with bureaucrats as they have to do in bigger companies,' says John Scolaspico, Marmon's sales director. 'I can make decisions and deals with customers without referring back to head office.'

Marmons are now legends of longevity, the darlings of owner–operators, and not just in the United States. The company's biggest single order came from the Watania poultry farm in Saudi Arabia. This 'world apart', which produces a million eggs a day, ordered 400 trucks and precipitated a rash of orders throughout the Middle East. Small really can be beautiful.

OSHKOSH – A GREAT SURVIVOR

THERE AREN'T MANY like Oshkosh. The firm was formed in 1917 and is still going strong, still independent, still firmly based in the little town of the same name in the mid-western state of Wisconsin, a few miles south of Clintonville.

It all started with William R. Besserlich and Bernard A. Mosling, engineer and salesman respectively. Besserlich had been a pioneer of four-wheel-drive cars, initially called Badgers before the firm changed its name to Four Wheel Drive Auto Company in 1911. In 1913 Besserlich sold his shares in FWD to Mosling and they started up on their own. Their major assets were Besserlich's patents. The first covered the transfer of power to all four wheels by means of an automatic locking differential in the transfer case. The other greatly improved the steering and drive capability of the front driving axle. In 1916 these represented a revolution, greatly enhancing the qualities and handling of four-wheel-drive vehicles. Even Mosling's considerable persuasive talents couldn't convince other manufacturers to take up the idea, so in early 1917 they raised $50,000 (£33,334) to build a truck – Old Betsy, which is still proudly displayed at the company's headquarters in Oshkosh, whose citizens had subscribed most of the money.

Their first production truck, the Model A, had a number of new features, including a door on

each side, a windshield and windows adjustable for ventilation. It was powered by a Herschel–Spillman four-cylinder engine which heated the fuel at three different points to get the most from the low-octane fuel of the day. One of the keys to Oshkosh's survival has been their continuing reliance on engines bought from outside.

It was the four-wheel drive that distinguished the Model A from the 100 or so other vehicles being manufactured in Wisconsin at the time. Nevertheless, sales were sluggish and in 1922 Besserlich was eased out of the top job by Mosling.

Sales reached a mere twenty-three vehicles in 1924 but the company was rescued the six-cylinder Model H introduced the next year. This became a favourite of local municipalities for road construction and snow removal (Mosling used to rub his hands at the sight of the first flakes, 'pennies from heaven', he called them).

He did not rely on snow removal alone, however. Apart from specialities like fire engines, trucks for logging and road-building, and even mobile grocery stores, the standard truck was ideally suited for collecting the produce of the thousands of dairy farms in the mid west found at the ends of dusty, muddy, rutted cart tracks.

Inevitably, the Depression crippled the company and in 1930 it was reorganized and Mosling was consigned to the salesman's job. Three years later the TR was introduced – the first rubber-tyred earth-mover ever built. Oshkosh prospered as a maker of such specialized vehicles, and not only for civilian use: its first success with the military came with the more powerful and refined W Series which were found to be ideal as snow-blowers and dump trucks. The company did so well that in 1944 Mosling returned as president and retired only in 1956 (to be succeeded by his son John). The Moslings could now offer advanced 6x6 tractors, and in 1955 they brought out the 50-50, the first truck ever built for the specific purpose of hauling cement. These were refined (or rather, made more rugged) as the R Series for use in oil-fields in the Middle East.

Then came a renewal of the relationship with the US armed forces. This started with a military adaptation of one of the firm's standard products, the snow-blower. These trucks were adapted for the DEW line, the chain of early-warning radar stations in northern Canada, machines which also became favourites with managers of commercial airports. Then came the MB-5, an aircraft rescue and fire-fighting truck built for the US navy, and a series of aircraft-towing tractors which culminated in the 8x8 Heavy Expanded Mobility Tactical Trucks. HEMTTs were adaptable and consequently were used as cargo trucks, tankers, recovery vehicles and tractors for hauling Pioneer missile-launchers. Even the notoriously critical General Norman Schwarzkopf was impressed – he told a congressional committee: 'I am a great believer in the HEMTT.'

Oshkosh has never moved from its home town since it made its first truck, 'Old Betsy'. Note the importance attached to the fact that it was 'four-wheel drive'.

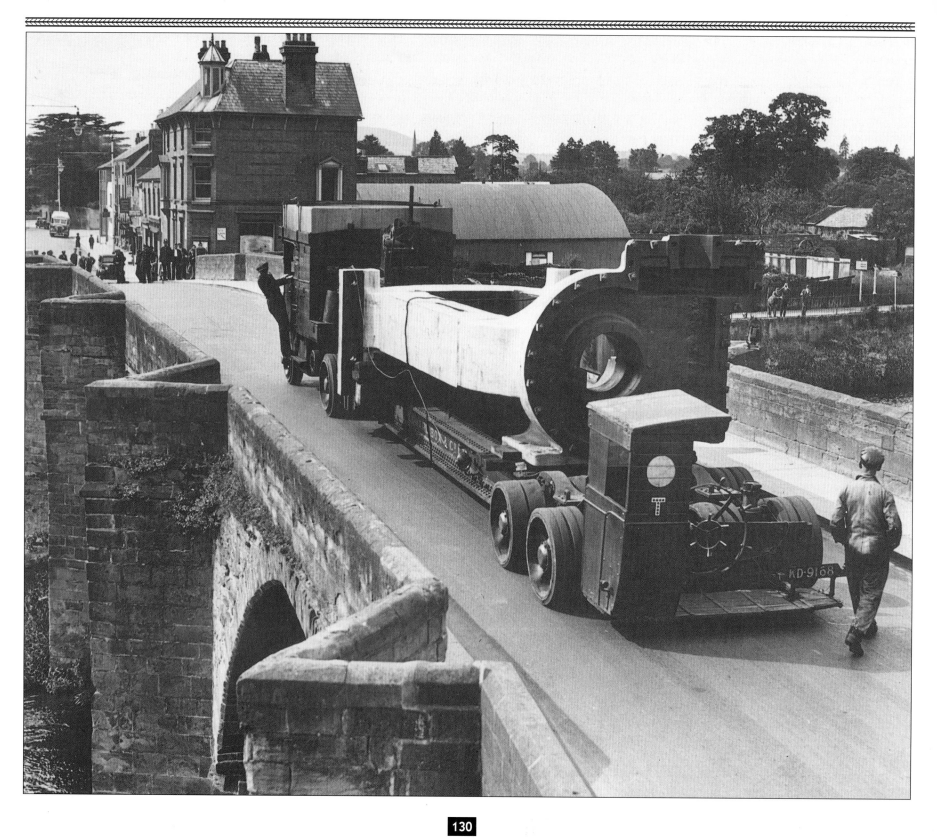

Chapter Eight

TRUCKS ON STEROIDS

BIG TRUCKS ARE SOMEHOW DIFFERENT. Most of them are simply scaled-up versions of normal vehicles: everything about them is simply . . . bigger, stronger. But mere scale does impose one major difference – big trucks require special skills. Driving them is a craft, a mystery in itself.

Such trucks were and are used simply because some loads consist of machinery too large and complicated to be manufactured except in enormous, indivisible lumps. In Britain, as in many other countries, the need for extra-heavy haulage began in the late nineteenth century, with the development of electric generating plant. As early as 1904 a steam traction engine was used to haul parts for a hydro-electric scheme from London to the highlands of Scotland, parts of which were too big for the railways' loading gauge. The roads had to be steel-plated and the bridges reinforced to take the weight, and the trip took a full five years.

The process has speeded up since then, although one legendary driver, Harry Bolam, once spent four days and nights carrying a battle tank the 250 miles from Vickers' Newcastle factory to Salisbury Plain. Bolam was one of an elite band of drivers (and their mates) who inevitably inspired a host of splendid stories, many of them more or less true – even the vocabulary was special, with its talk of box girders,

bolsters, clevis pins and the 'swan-neck' girder trailers used by the famous firm of Wynn's of Newport that are still in use today.

Among the heroes was Bill Jemison. Bob Tuck[1] writes:

Tees Viaduct at Middlesbrough is one crossing where the highway people demand a slow measured pace from heavy loads so that the bridge's foundations are not unduly disturbed. Bill Jemison used to take this opportunity to simply engage the hand throttle, point the Scammell straight, then go to the back of the crew cab and make a fresh brew of tea. After the initial shock, the escorting police motorcyclists became used to seeing a driverless Scammell coming towards them, but they never ventured too close to investigate because it was not unknown for them to be showered with cold tea when Bill threw out the contents preparatory to warming the pot!

For Jemison, as for most British drivers, the Scammell was the king of the road. G. Scammell and Nephew first exhibited a massive articulated truck at the Olympia Motor Show in 1921. It was so successful that the company moved out of London to Watford, where it remained until it fell victim to the recession and the corporate manoeuvrings of the 1980s,

(Opposite) An early Scammell carrying the first 100-ton load ever hauled by a petrol-driven engine on British roads.

Two Fowler steam wagons were required to haul the parts for a hydro-electric scheme across Rannoch Moor Scotland, in 1934.

although a few trucks continue to be made in the old works.

Although the seven and a half ton vehicle shown at Olympia demonstrated the importance of Scammell's innovatory ideas in designing articulated vehicles, it was the Pioneer, designed by the firm's engineering genius, Oliver North, and introduced six years later, which made the name world-famous. Its favourite configuration was as a 6x4 tractor or rigid six-wheeler, equally at home on mud, sand or the hilliest of roads. Its major distinguishing feature was not the engine (Scammell's own or the Gardner 6LW), or the six-speed gearbox, but the way power was distributed to the four rear wheels through a single

rear differential and a pair of conventional half-shafts: all the wheels received power but the arrangement allowed one wheel to be as much as two feet above its fellow on the other side without loss of traction, thanks to the intermeshing gear wheels.

Just as important was a cooling system with a row of wire-wound tubes, which provided an enormous cooling surface, topped by a large water pot (hence the regular wisp of steam and the nickname 'the coffee pot'). Whatever the angle, however high or low the temperature, the Scammell never boiled over – even in the Iraqi desert, where it proved its worth hauling the pipes for the pipeline built in the 1930s from the oilfields to the Mediterranean.

In the early 1950s, the Pioneer was replaced by the Explorer, powered by a Meadows petrol engine, which military customers preferred to diesel. The takeover by Leyland in 1955 merely provided Scammell with more capital to compete with the Thornycroft Antar, which had taken its market in the early postwar years. The result was the Constructor, powered by a Rolls-Royce C6NFL diesel, which could produce 200bhp at 2,200rpm. The Constructor had up to twelve different gear ratios and a suspension far stronger than that designed for the Pioneer. The only feature not worthy of the firm was the cab, a hand-me-down from one of the lightweight Bedfords then

going out of production. The Constructor and its bigger brother, the Super-Constructor, which boasted a semi-automatic eight-speed box and was rated at a modest 180 tons (183 tonnes), remained in production until 1981.

They had to share the glory with the Contractor, which had the advantage of using the engines made by Cummins in Britain since 1956 (or the Rolls-Royce 12.17-litre 300bhp Eagle diesel) as well as a fifteen-speed Fuller gearbox, which could perform at up to 240 tons (244 tonnes) total weight.

Such vehicles often had long and strange lives. One ERF eight-wheeler, known to the licensing authorities as ABT 738, but to its devotees as Two-Ton Tessie (named after well-loved comedienne Two-Ton Tessie O'Shea), was originally a six-

Mack always specialized in trucks for use in the construction industry.

wheeler. After 1945 it was converted into an eight-wheeler and fitted with a Scammell turntable to help it carry long steel bars. A 240-ton (244-tonne) Contractor, stretched to 38ft (11.6m) to carry some American-made transformers, became known as 'Big Goody' (it was the largest truck in Goodfellows' fleet) and went on to work in Saudi Arabia.

Roads impose their own weight limits, but off-road vehicles can be as heavy, as specialized and as extraordinary as the user requires. They are used for a bewildering variety of purposes in a range of sites whose only common factor is the extraordinary strains they impose on the machines. The most obvious and numerous are the bulldozer, the excavator, the skimmer (in which a bucket slides along a boom) and the drag line which makes shallow cuts in soft earth or sand. But the sector is specialized enough to absorb a wide variety of monsters designed for specific uses, most obviously to build roads – like the

The Sno-cat is still made by the Tucker family in the little Oregon town of Salem. This one was used by Dr Vivian Fuchs in the first motorized Trans-Antarctic journey in 1957.

This Scammell contract is
actually inside a Welsh
mountain, hauling one of
the 120-foot-long pipes
required for the Dinorwic
pumped-storage
hydro-electric scheme.

By 1950 towers for oil refineries – in this case travelling from Teeside to Mexico – had joined machinery destined for power stations as super-heavy loads requiring careful handling through cities like Manchester.

Euclid's earth-movers – and to strip-mine coal and other minerals, like the Ruston & Bucyrus drag lines.

Even the best names in highway trucks – Kenworth, Peterbilt or Scammell – find it difficult, if not impossible, to cope with the problems of size, although Mack's rigid high-sided trucks were always a favourite among operators of open-cast coal mines. So the names involved – Perlini, Kockum, Euclid, Lectrahaul, Wabco and, above all, Caterpillar – are little known outside their own esoteric world.

Once the need for these vehicles to move on roads is removed, all sorts of technical possibilities open up. The tyres, for instance, are so squashy that there is no need for much in the way of suspension; the shock absorbers also double as steering kingpins. But size also brings problems. Perhaps the worst is the transmission: in the past so much of the power even from the massive fifty-litre engines used, was absorbed by the sheer mass required by a conventional prop and drive shafts that the engine generated power for electric motors on each axle. But recently Caterpillar has succeeded in producing orthodox gearboxes and transmissions that solve the problem and are more efficient than separate drive.

Naturally, in this sphere of superlatives, there is competition for the biggest truck in the world. One well-publicized contender for the title is the 'crawler transport' that moves the Space Shuttle to its launch pad at Cape Kennedy at a stately 1mph (1.6kph). Other less well-known SPTs (Self Propelled Trailers) use the same formula, of a petrol or diesel engine generating electricity for the motors. But the undoubted champion is the Terex Titan, weighing in at over 600 tons (610 tonnes) loaded, and powered by a 3,300bhp engine. Only one was ever made. Even off-the-road size has its limits.

(Opposite) The most glamorous, and slowest, of land vehicles. The Crawler-Transporter, 20 feet (6.1 metres) high and over 130 feet (40 metres) long, and weighing 2,700 tons (2,743 tonnes) used to haul the space shuttle Columbia to its launch pad at a steady 1 mph.

Sources

CHAPTER 1

1. Prince Marshall, *Lorries, Trucks and Vans* (Blandford Press, London, England), 1972.
2. Maurice Kelly, *The Undertype Steam Road Wagon* (Goose Publishing, Cambridge, England), 1975.
3. *Commercial Motor* (UK) 16 June, 1933.
4. *Commercial Motor* (UK) 20 December, 1968.

CHAPTER 2

1. Robert Tuck, *The Golden Days of Heavy Haulage*, (Roundoak Publishing, Wellington, England), 1992.

CHAPTER 3

1. Quoted by Lucien Chanuc in *Camions, Chronique d'un Siècle* (Editions MDM, Paris, France), 1993.
2. Maurice Kelly, op. cit.
3. Bill Aldridge, *The Mechanical Horse* (The Mechanical Horse Club, Chesterfield, England), 1992.

CHAPTER 4

1. John Hibbs, *The History of British Bus Services* (David & Charles, Newton Abbot, England), 1968.
2. John Hibbs, op. cit.
3. John Hibbs, op. cit.
4. John Hibbs, op. cit.
5. John Hibbs, op. cit.
6. *London Mercury* (as quoted in O.E.D.).
8. Gavin Booth, *Classic Buses* (Frazer Stewart, Oxfordshire, England), 1993.
9. Gavin Booth, op. cit.
10. Lucien Chanuc, op. cit.
11. Maurice Kelly, op. cit.
12. Maurice Kelly, op. cit.

13. T.C. Barker and Michael Robbins, *The History of London Transport* (Allen & Unwin, London, England), 1976.
14. T.C. Barker and Michael Robbins, op. cit.
15. *Independent*, 22 September, 1994.
16. Oscar Schisgall, *The Greyhound Story* (J.G. Ferguson, Chicago, USA), 1985.

CHAPTER 5

1. Chris Ellis, *Military Transport of World War I* (Blandford Press, London, England), 1970.
2. Chris Ellis, op. cit.
3. N.M. Cary Jnr, *The Use of Motor Vehicles in the US Army, 1899–1939* (Altus, Georgia, USA), 1986.
4. Captain C.R. Kutz, *War on Wheels* (Lane, London, England), 1941.
5. Brian Baxter, *Breakdown, A History of Recovery Vehicles in the British Army*, (H.M.S.O., London, England), 1989.
6. N.M. Cary Jnr, op. cit.
7. Brian Baxter, op. cit.
8. Jean-Gabriel Jeudy, *The Jeep* (Haynes, Yeovil, England), 1981.

CHAPTER 6

1. Bart Vanderveen, *Fire-Fighting Vehicles 1840–1950* (Haynes, Yeovil, England), 1992.

CHAPTER 7

1. John Gunnell (ed.), *American Work Trucks* (Krause Publications, Wisconsin, USA), 1993.

CHAPTER 8

1. Robert Tuck, *The Supertrucks of Scammell*, (Fitzjames, London, England), 1987.

Index

*(Numbers in **bold** refer to illustrations)*

Picture Credits

Boxtree would like to thank the private individuals, companies and picture agencies who have provided the pictures and photographs in this book, and by courtesy of whom they are reproduced. Credits are by pages number.

Nick Baldwin: 6, 10, 12, 14, 16 (top), 17, 18, 20, 21, 26, 30–31, 36, 38, 45 (top and bottom), 52, 54, 57, 60, 63, 64, 68, 71, 72, 73, 87, 105, 106, 108 (bottom), 112, 113, 114, 115, 120, 122, 123, 133; **Ford Motor Company:** 50, 51 (bottom); **Hulton Deutsch Collection:** 8–9, 24, 28, 35, 44, 46-7; **Imperial War Museum:** 84, 85, 86, 90 (top), 92, 94, 96–7, 101; **London Transport Museum:** 76; **Marmon Motorcompany:** 127; **Mercedes–Benz:** 39, 40, 41; **NASA (National Aeronautics and Space Administration):** 138; **The National Motor Museum, Beaulieu:** 2, 22, 51 (top), 66 (bottom), 82, 100, 118, 121, 126; **Oshkosh Truck Corporation:** 98, 128–9; **Quadrant:** 23, 32, (top and bottom), 33, 37; **Range/Bettmann/UPI:** 116–17, 119; **The Science Museum/Science & Society Picture Library:** 1, 62, 136–7; **Telegraph Colour Library:** 79, 110, 124; **Topham:** 34, 42, 49, 53, 58, 61, 66 (top), 67, 69, 74–5, 80, 81, 88, 89, 90 (bottom), 91, 95, 102, 104, 107, 108 (top), 109; **Robert Tuck:** 13, 16, 19 (bottom), 130, 132, 135; **Tucker Sno-cat Corporation:** 134.